Ponder 2021
Annual Collection of Poem Reviews

Ashok Subramanian

Ponder Publications

ISBN-13:9798814895707

Cover design by: Art Painter
Library of Congress Control Number: 2018675309
Printed in the United States of America

TO HIM, I SURRENDER.

Dedicated to

To my mother, Saroja
(21.08.1944 - 02.12.2021)
And

The Poets
Whose Poems
I had the privilege
To Review
In 2021

CONTENTS

ACKNOWLEDGEMENT

2021 was a tumultuous year. I lost my father-in-law in April and my mother in December. I did not write any reviews between September and December after my mother passed away.

I thank my family – my wife Gayathri and my son Anirudh, and my brother Rajesh for helping my way through.

What kept me going on Ponder 2021 was my tribe – Elizabeth Urabe and Desiree Driesenaar, and my friend and creative advisor, Shweta Hitesh Joshi. I thank you for helping me hold the steering wheel on a bumpy ride.

The book would not have been possible, had I not found the gems that I always search for in the deep sea. It is a magical journey that I had endeavored for the second year, and I found the gems.

The pillars of this book are the poets who wrote contemporary poems that touch and tear our hearts and souls and heal them. These are poems published on LinkedIn and I took their consent to reproduce, review and publish. This effort aims to create a bread crumb trail that captures these poems and poets through a publication. A published book is a legacy of literature. My eternal gratitude to these poets who made this possible. My editing efforts have been solo considering the line-up for this year.

I thank Amazon and Kindle for making my efforts easier.

Ponder 2021 is a labor of love and brings together poets across continents in one book. I hope that you enjoy this collection of reviews for this year. Hope to bring around Ponder 2022 as well.

~Ashok Subramanian

1. MOTHERHOOD THROUGH THE CHILD'S EYE

Mom! Mother! Amma! Ai! Ammi! Mummy! Maa!

The above are the variants of the first and the most powerful word a child utters as soon as it is born.

We all know why. Mothers are the noblest of all beings. Their sacrifice in giving birth and nurturing their children is of untold value.

The first review of this year, 2021, where hope lies for the end of the pandemic, starts with where it all begins-Motherhood and Childhood.

Life, in particular childhood, is shaped by ingredients and incidents. Ingredients of the child come from their genetic makeup. Incidents come from the events and responses throughout childhood. The formative years, in turn, shape the rest of our lives.

Parents are the most important influencers who contribute to both the incidents and ingredients. They are always the participants in the first sights and sounds, food and love. In particular, mothers are the first love and parent of a child, showering their children with unconditional love. The sacrifice of their lives and priorities for their children's upbringing are stories of unparalleled wonder.

How do these children view their mothers? As they grow up, their mother's lives become their memories.

> "But there's a story behind everything. How a picture got on a wall. How a scar got on your face. Sometimes the stories are simple, and sometimes they are hard and heart-breaking. But behind all your stories is always your mother's story, because hers is where yours begins."
> — Mitch Albom, For One More Day

These memories make the stories. Some memories morph into poems. In this review, I am happy to bring along two powerful poems of those memories, 'I also fought' by Adedoyin Olaleye- and 'A Chapati of Resilience' by Parneet Kaur.

Both poems shine the light on motherhood through the protagonist's — the child's eye. In the first poem, a child her mother's death during her birth. The child sees the struggles of her mother during her birth as a fight for life. In her own unspoken words, she screams about her right to live, while people misunderstood her as the cause behind her mother's demise.

In the second poem, another child from Punjab, India portrays how her character is shaped by her mother's tough love. The resilience, thinking, and character of this child evolve under her mother's watchful eye.

The struggles of the mothers in the poems are portrayed by their children. The children see their mothers' struggles and paint their perspectives in these beautiful poems. Both poems reflect the reality of today's mothers and are not utopian in any form. The verses crawl into our hearts and stir our souls.

Here we go. Our first poem of 2021!

Poem 1: I Also Fought

Figure 1 I also fought. Image by F. Muhammad from Pixabay

It was night
It was the middle of it
Mother fought
She fought hard
I sat back
Mother cried
Tears washed her eyes
I sat back
I wished I could cry too

She screamed
I couldn't
She trembled
I was mute

Mother held tightly to the bedpost
I held strongly to the big hope
Mother! Hold still. I'll soon behold

Blood gushed
Chord cut

She hung faintly to fate
I clutched firmly at my fist
Prayers escaped my nostrils
She gasped
I cried
She convulsed
I thought I fought...

It was night
It was the middle of it
Mother fought
But she could not

Mother left
I was left
People wept
and felt
I made her dead

But I did not
and I thought they saw
that life is war
that I also fought

~Adedoyin Olaleye

Commentary on Poem 1:

I was torn between picturing a slightly older child witnessing childbirth or a child watching its birth — I went for the latter because of the conclusion of the poem.

Imagine a child seeing itself born, and in the process, observing her mother's struggles and fighting the world's partisan opinion. Poet Adedoyin Olaleye has composed this graphic and touching poem 'I also fought'.

> It was night
> It was the middle of it
> Mother fought
> She fought hard
> I sat back
> Mother cried
> Tears washed her eyes
> I sat back
> I wished I could cry too

The scene opens like this: It is a night like no other, in the life of the mother and child. The mother is in the middle of childbirth. The pain and the effort bring tears to her eyes.

'Mother *fought, she fought hard*' — the repetition of '*fought*' indicates an emphasis on what the mother is going through. Then 'mother *cried, tears washed her eyes*' — in the fight, emotions, and efforts are spilling out as tears.

The child is overwhelmed as it sees that in its birth, her mother is struggling and fighting the pain. The child realizes that she cannot do anything, but can only wish she could cry. The child actually would have cried, but for the outside world, the cries might be the typical baby cries. The bystanders or helpers won't understand the child's painful response to her mother's struggles. More on them in due course.

> She screamed
> I couldn't
> She trembled
> I was mute
>
> Mother held tightly to the bedpost
> I held strongly to the big hope
> Mother! Hold still... I'll soon behold

The struggle of the mother increases multi-fold. The pain manifests into convulsions. It is intolerable. '*Screaming and trembling*' and '*holding tightly to the bed post*' — the child's mother fights hard. The child is agonized by this suffering, which is multiplying by the minute. She tries to scream, but cannot, because she is mute — her head and body are being pushed out. She can feel her mother as she slowly sleeps through the uterus to the vaginal canal. The push of her mother to extricate her child is felt by her.

Then comes a beautiful little conversation! — *'Mother! Hold still... I'll soon behold'*. The child, even if it cannot speak and is mute, gives hope to her mother, that she will behold this extra-ordinary moment in her life — her birth.

The imagination of the poet rides deep — the first of this world the child sees is the struggle of the only person she knows.

> Blood gushed
> Chord cut
> She hung faintly to fate
> I clutched firmly at my fist
> Prayers escaped my nostrils
> She gasped
> I cried
> She convulsed
> I thought I fought...

The struggles increase. The midwife or the doctor cuts the cord — the umbilical cord, the last physical connection between the child and the mother, and blood gushes out. The world changes at that moment for the yet-to-be-born child. The child starts moving away from and out of her mother.

The efforts have the mother down and out, and the remaining life seeps away by the loss of blood. As the helpless onlooker, the child realizes that her mother is fighting a losing battle. She clenches her fist and prays through her nostrils.

Imagine the first breath that you take has to be a prayer. A bloody scene it is. Then her most loved person is slipping away. Then she inhales the air of this planet.

This is more than baptism by fire. This is torture by birth. An immeasurable struggle. The child 'thinks' that she fought too. Indeed, my child. Indeed, you did. But wait. There is more to come.

> It was night
> It was the middle of it
> Mother fought
> But she could not
>
> Mother left
> I was left

Finally, the end comes for the mother. The poet slides to the background, the time — it is still the middle of the night. A short period, but an eternity for the mother. The few moments are a lifetime for the child.

The mother fights but she cannot fight further. She does not give up till the end. She gives everything to get her child out of her womb into this world. She leaves, leaving the child alone in this world. A pervading sense of loss seeps into our minds.

The wordplay with 'left' is beautiful. A small tickle of brilliance in such an emotional and larger-than-life moment.

> People wept
> and felt
> I made her dead
>
> But I did not
> and I thought they saw
> that life is war
> that I also fought

People around the child's mother weep — weep in sorrow, condoling a death that came too soon. Then they look at the newborn child. The child feels the prick of the stares that blame her for her mother's death.

Society will never understand. But the child gives them the benefit of the doubt that makes them half less malicious than they are. The child just has seen her mother fight for her life and has come into this world, fighting for her birth. So, in its short life, the child realizes that 'life is war'. And, she also fought.

I bite my tongue and grind my teeth. My eyes are teary and my mouth is dry. The effect of the short moments of her birth leaves a deep imprint on the fresh mind of the child as she sees the struggles of her mother, and her birth, and finally the partisan views of the people around him.

"If you can't go back to your mother's womb, you'd better learn to be a good fighter."
— **Anchee Min, Red Azalea**

The world is a beautiful place, but for some, it starts as a struggle. Poet Adedoyin has owownedur hearts with these deep, deep verses.

Poem 2: 'A Chapati of Resilience'

Figure 2 my mother made me … Image by chitsu san from Pixabay

My mother made me
    like a chapati,
    shaped me uniformly,
    sudden necessary beatings
    with roller
    to flatten my surface of thinking.

Made me perfect
    home-made solution
    for everyone's hunger.

She rose me like an aerated balloon
    of resilience,
    applying adequate pressure
    to help me grow.

The process requires patience,
    a born gift from and to mother

but little did she know,
    I had intolerance of my father,
    the fire in my soul,
    the bubble inside my lips and
    the pressure of my black wounds
    would one day burst at her own hands.

    ~Parneet Kaur

Commentary on Poem 2:
How does a child become what she is today?

Let us go back to Ingredients, Incidents, and Influencers. Mother is the first and the primary influencer, alright. Poet Parneet Kaur brings out how a mother shapes her child with humor and lividity and a dash of ethnicity. Parneet Kaur is from Punjab, India, and that influences her composition.

    My mother made me
    like a chapatti,
    shaped me uniformly,
    sudden necessary beatings
    with roller
    to flatten my surface of thinking.

*Figure 3 Sudden necessary beatings with a roller (in the picture,
Image by congerdesign from Pixabay)*

Punjabi mothers roll the wheat dough with a wooden roller. It is a skill that is passed on from generation to generation. The roller, beyond the rolls, is also a wieldy weapon, especially when the kitchen queens become angry. With a barrage of choicest words, the roller sends a message to those outside the kitchen, whether it is the child or the man.

The girl's thinking - round, uniform, and flat - has been shaped by the mother's oversight and the occasional beatings.

'*To flatten the surface of my thinking*' has two layers —primary and obvious humour, and a subtle acknowledgment of her mother's influence on her thinking. A perfect metaphor for tough love.

The beatings are '*sudden and necessary*'. Chapatis are circular dry slices of bread, shaped after mashing and rolling. The dough's ingredients — wheat, water, and salt, resulting in great taste. The roller shapes the dough into perfect circular chapatis, in the most capable hands of the Punjabi mom.

Are the beatings necessary? Can they not be just words of admonition? Parenting in this part of the world has to be understood. The underlying emotion is love and concern, and not anger or inability. In large families, the women are busy cooking enormous meals for the entire family. Childcare is part of multitasking, and that requires quick and decisive responses to potentially quirky situations that the child is in.

Punjabi moms are as much temperamental as loving. *'Sudden and necessary'* beatings are the outcome of the mom's response to the situation caused by the child's behaviour.

I am shaped by my mother's tough love too. In a moment, I lost two teeth; but gained a lot of wisdom. Never repeated the mistake. The stick was never spared. The child was never spoiled.

> Made me perfect
> home-made solution
> for everyone's hunger.

The outcome of such tough love is the conditioning ahead of the life situation that comes along the girl's way. One way of looking at a 'home-*made solution for everyone's hunger*' is the ability of the women to handle the problems thrown at them by the family, including cooking and childcare. In a large family, that is a humungous task.

We need to move the last stanza forward to understand the next metaphor.

> But little did she know,
> I had intolerance of my father,
> the fire in my soul,
> the bubble inside my lips and...

Under the hood of the car — the child, there are the father's qualities. Intolerance, fieriness, and a bit of haughtiness *(the bubble inside my lips)*. Father's love is more mellowed and softer towards the girl child. So the copycat attitudes seep in naturally.

The girl, like her father, throws attitude at the woman of the house, the mother. The entitlement comes from being the recipient of unabashed love and care, albeit tough. The men fear and respect the women, for, without them, they are parentless children.

> She rose me like an aerated balloon
> of resilience,
> applying adequate pressure
> to help me grow.

When the shaped and flattened chapatis cook in the *Tava* (the oven), they inflate due to the evaporating water bubbles trapped inside, like a balloon. The skin puffs because of the heat like an *'aerated balloon'*. The heat — a metaphor for the subtle and constant conditioning by the mother, makes the child shaped into a *'homemade solution'*.

> The pressure of my black wounds
> would one day burst at her own hands.

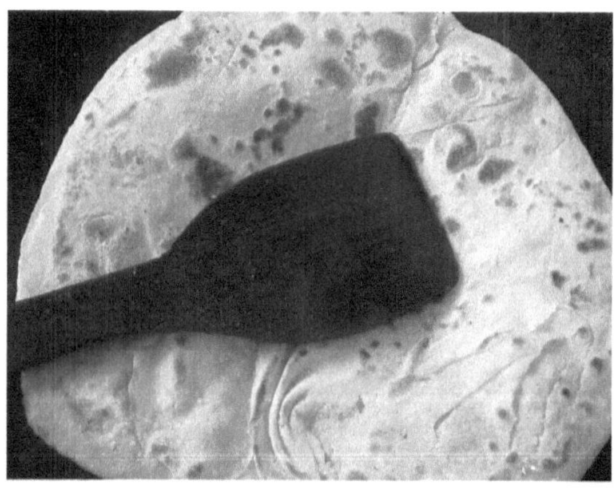

Figure 4 Chapati on a tava (oven)

The black spots are burnt parts of the skin of the chapati that burst due to the fissures created by heat. As one side is enough exposed to the heat, the chapati is turned over to the other side by the skilful hands of the mother. The skin bursts and the hot air escapes like a bursting aerated balloon.

The entitlement of a kid meets the tough love of a parent.

> The process requires patience,
> a born gift from and to mother

To be constantly at it, the mother can never lose patience and hope. She knows she is the last line of life for the child.

The poem, written from the child's perspective, also brings out her maturity and self-awareness, and the acknowledgment of her mother's contribution to shaping her character. And when her turn comes to be a mother, she would be ready.

Finally, this poem is an ode to the tough love of Punjabi moms who are the single reason for creating the world's largest 'giving' community, the Punjabis.

Figure 5 Pic Courtesy: Ryan Christopher Jones for the New York Times

The Sikh Centre of New York, in Queens Village, has served more than 145,000 free meals in the last two months, as part of their faith tradition of feeding anyone in need. No one ever is hungry under the benevolence and care of a Punjabi, anywhere in the world. From New York to New Delhi, Punjabi mom's tough love has created this culture of giving and caring, without any fuss and bias. Visit them in one of their 'langars', you can see the success stories.

Conclusion:

The poems are contrasting. The first poem is about childbirth and the second is about childhood. The first poem brings out the mother's desperate struggles but still teaches the child about the 'war of life', while the second poem brings out the mother's long-drawn battle to condition the child to make it a giver.

The similarity is the mature narrative and the deep understanding that the children share about their mother's struggles, sacrifices, and intent. Poets Adedoyin Olaleye and Parneet Kaur end the poems with the social views of the children amid the contrasting tales and settings.

I leave the readers to discern and discover the poems. I am now thinking of my mother and childhood.

~Ashok Subramanian

2. FLITS OF FREEDOM

The summer of 2021 is here — there is no spring in the tropics. But the heat is hardly making news. A fresh wave of the COVID19 virus is gripping many nations, including India.

COVID19 has restricted the free flow of humans across cities, states, and nations. Travel is freedom and freedom is what humans cherish.

But as March unravelled, many of my family members and I have fallen into the virus. The mandatory 14-day quarantine has begun. Already familiar with the lock-ins during the lockdowns, we entered the isolation stage.

Fatigue and fever took over the first week. The second week is a slow recovery. My mind is scattered but I am not keen to pick up the pieces. I do the must-be-done — some video conference calls & some poetry reading-writing.

'The virus entered my ribcage

And my nest became my cage'.

Figure 6 'The virus entered my ribcage, and my nest became my cage'.

I wonder how life has changed in a year. Last year, we were looking at closing out the financial year, and the world crashed all around us. People limped their way towards the New Year to chase their livelihoods, but the second wave reminds us that freedom comes at a cost.

As I recuperate at my home, the freedom I yearn for leads me to the search for poems. Freedom is never absolute. Humans are social animals, and society is a bond. My exploration of freedom is contextual but open-minded. I stare at the sky and the tall trees and look for their limitlessness. I look at the birds that fly and rest on them and look for their liberty. But even more, I look for my liberation in poetic verses.

Poet Donovan Baldwin's 'Cardinal', and Poet Sourabha Rao's 'Liberation' bring much joy as we explore freedom through a kaleidoscope. Freedom is sometimes a fleeting thought or a flicker of vision. A world that is out there brings the feeling of freedom within.

'Cardinal' brings out the vision of freedom and consumption of the feeling within. It provides a fleeting glimpse of a cardinal, a red bird, against the still slow-changing dawn landscape, like a ripple in a still pond. That is the glimpse of freedom.

'Liberation' cleaves the moment at which a bud opens and how time escapes from darkness to light. This is a short but deep poem, bringing in that little flitting movement of freedom in that moment of transience.

Most of us would have seen these flits of freedom happen in front of our eyes, but these are trapped in the verses of these two magnificent poems. Please join me in enjoying the two freeze-frame moments.

Poem 1: Cardinal

Walking in the park at dawn
*   a flitting bird did see.*
*   A cardinal flew across my path*
*   as red as red can be.*

Flickering flame in dawn's soft light
*   Set the day ablaze for me.*
*   Trapped within my own gray cage*
*   I was happy he was free.*

~Donovan Baldwin

Commentary on Poem 1:

Donovan is a natural rhymer. His world is a combination of simple events and feelings, yet filled with subtlety. When he sees the most loved red bird of the continent, the cardinal, he feels inspired and yet happy. Why?

Let us look at the cardinal, the bird. I quote National Geographic[1] here. It says 'The northern cardinal is so well-loved that it has been named the official bird of no fewer than seven U.S. states. Bright red cardinals are easily identified by even casual bird watchers; and are often seen frequenting backyards and bird feeders. Cardinals are active songbirds and sing a variety of different melodies.'

The setting of the poem is when the sun breaks out in the eastern sky. A blushing orange dawn skyscape opens. The poet, who loves his coffee (I have the privilege of following Donovan's posts on his coffee and walks), ambles along in a park. He sees a *flitting* bird. Cardinals are never known to be still. They always hop, flutter, and fly.

Seeing them reminds me of another poem I reviewed last year, called the 'Wren'[2]), one may feel the Schrodinger's effect. A 'flitting' glimpse -here and there.

The poet sees the Cardinal flying across his path. His eyes catch the Cardinal's appearance -'*as red as red can be*'. It is red in its most glorious form - deep, unabashed red. Can red be redder? No, Red wears best on the Cardinal.

Mornings walks are about opening our minds to a new day ahead — a combination of fresh air and discovery. Putting myself in the poet's shoes, I try to watch this gorgeous sight of seeing a day being born, the stillness of the morning air, and this — the flitting red event — a hopping and fluttering Cardinal — is a mark of life, symbolizing the soul of the earth. Why do I feel this?

> Flickering flame in dawn's soft light
> Set the day ablaze for me.

The birth of the dawn, young and fragile, with its '*soft light*', a mellowed event, is changed by the red fluttering bird. Suddenly, there is that rush of purpose and adrenalin — the Cardinal '*sets the day ablaze*' for the poet.

I did not miss the transition of the poet from an 'observer' to an 'inspired', in that flitting moment. The world needs inspiration and this flitting moment of the glimpse of the red bird is no less.

The poet is not done yet. Wait for the last lines.

> Trapped within my own grey cage
> I was happy he was free.

The poet ruminates about his life — he is now and trapped in his 'grey cage', an indication of his aging body, but also a life that has been spent in bonds of his country, society, and family, that he has tried to unshackle through his verses.

Notwithstanding his situation, he is *happy* to see that the 'cardinal' *is free*. Only an emancipated soul can appreciate freedom, and that too, the freedom of others — the freedom that nature provides.

Nature also has bonds, but those are symbiotic. As an observer, as an inspired, as a trapped soul yet appreciating, the poet has brought forth this symbiotic relationship between freedom and nature, in a simple yet subtle expression of his happiness.

The poem also reflects the harmony of how a human can fit into nature — breaking dawn and a flitting little red bird. Just be there and take it all in. And maybe, if one can, like the poet, be inspired, enjoy the moment and be happy.

I wonder why the poet is feeling that he is trapped in his *own grey cage*. I almost missed this in the joy of visualizing the red bird. The words carry a lot of weight, the weight of regret.

Could the poet have lived a free life? What shackled him? Why has he not broken out? Or does he talk about the larger human society — sunk in a pile of chained bodies and souls, unable to unleash their wanton desires and wanderlust? The questions remain.

The poet may be stuck in this shackled world, yet happy to see the Cardinal free. A point to ponder for me and the reader.

Poem 2: Liberation

Figure 7 when the bud opened her eyes ... Image by Pezibear from Pixabay

When the bud opened her eyes
the time trapped in her
spilled from darkness to light.

~Sourabha Rao

Commentary on Poem 2:

Nature has its miraculous ways of showing how freedom is symbiotic. Freedom is a kinetic action, driven by movements.

"Those who do not move, do not notice their chains."
— Rosa Luxemburg

The movement of the breeze, the rustling of leaves, the crashing of waves, the rising and setting of sun and moon, the flutter of butterflies and the birds, all capture freedom in its profound state — movement. This transition also leads to transformation.

The poet captures the magic of movement or transition as a statement of freedom and a message of liberation.

When the bud opened her eyes

A bud is a flower in its formative stage with its small petals folded. The growth of the flower happens inside the closed petals. Imagine this like a mother's womb. Inside the womb is a dark universe, where life is formed and grows.

The inside of the bud is where the flower's ingredients, including the filament and anther, which contains pollen — the seed for future species, develop to form the core of the flower. This happens away from the sunlight.

The beauty of life is both within; when it is formed in the deep, dark universe of its own, and without, when it explodes into the universe as the young one of the species. This transition is what the poet captures in those words *when the bud opened her eyes.*

This is the birthing process of the flower. The first part, where the prenatal growth that happens inside is analogical to the bud closing its eyes, captures the whole new world within. So when it *'opens its eyes'*, the world underneath explodes, like the Bing Bang explosion of the universe.

The time trapped in her

A bit of science here. Humans cannot still understand the time before Bing Bang. We call the exact moment of Bing Bang t=0. Similarly, the time at which the bud opens its eyes, is t=0, the birth of time in that little flower universe.

If one can understand the profundity of these words, it is enlightening, to say the least. Each flower bud opening is a Big Bang event itself, in its flower universe.

Spilled from darkness to light

Science continues but is camouflaged as poetry. The light trapped inside that tiny bud now explodes and travels out, spilling new imagery. From t=0, it is the escape of light and matter with it, that makes this universe. Time itself comes into definition after the Big Bang event — the bud opening its eyes. Time hidden in the dark, in the womb of the bud, is now out with the larger universe.

If you are an observer, you can observe this little event in the gardens and forests, in the plants and trees, and everywhere around. Myriad universes explode open, letting pockets of time escape from the darkness of the floral wombs into the light of the larger universe. Why do scientists then look for answers far away? Our poet has found it very close to us.

Each Big Bang is its act of freedom, letting time escape from darkness to light. It happens in a flitting moment during the simple unravelling of the bud's petals.

You might not have seen this insight so far, but you might now. The verses of the poet bring to us a profound lesson in science, but more than that, the words of freedom, of the liberation of the arrested moment to fly free.

Flits of Freedom:

In our lives, we are inspired by events — events that do not mean much at a passing glance, but when our minds arrest those flitting moments, they manifest into deeper meanings.

Freedom is for those who seek, and for the seeker, there is a meaning to make. A cardinal flying in the poet's path during his morning way at dawn, or a bud opening in a garden are daily events. But when their minds seek answers from the events that they have observed, they turn into verses with profound meaning, capturing those flits of freedom.

I salute Poets Donovan Baldwin and Sourabha Rao for providing the opportunity to review these poems, and liberating me out of my caged stint, as I recuperate from COVID19.

~Ashok Subramanian

3. IDENTITY AND PURPOSE

Identity is a question that we try to seek answers to from both within and without. If you seek your identity without, then it is a sum of expectations of all people around you.

> "Nothing of me is original. I am the combined effort of everyone I've ever known."
> — Chuck Palahniuk, Invisible Monsters

We see how nature seeks its identity in the two poems we bring out in this review. One is from 'without', expectations of others, carried on shoulders of its meandering flow from its origin to the estuary. Poet Shweta Hitesh Joshi explores the burden of expectations and definitions given by others and how those bear down on the soul-search of the river in her poem 'The River'.

The second one is from 'within', an entity that knows its calling and therefore is sure and confident within.

> "My friend, I am not what I seem. Seeming is but a garment I wear — a care-woven garment that protects me from thy questionings and thee from my negligence. The "I" in me, my friend, dwells in the house of silence, and therein it shall remain forever more, unperceived, unapproachable."
> — Khalil Gibran, the Madman

The perception of eternity and stillness in the inner 'I' which is the identity that everybody tries to seek in their lives is achieved when one peels the layers of facades — clothes, undergarments, skin, muscle, and bones, and somewhere inside your heart and mind, or wherever the soul resides, a small bundle of thought that is embedded, is the place where we can see the identity.

How does one see this from Nature's perspective? The answer

is above us. Poet Elizabeth Urabe, in this second poem titled 'I am' brings this out beautifully in a triplet.

Poem 1: 'The River'

Figure 8 nobody asks a river... Image by Larisa Koshkina from Pixabay

Why nobody asks a river

If she gets tired

Of crossing jungles and mountains

Of flowing through bridges and between the cities

(Why nobody asks a river)

If she really wants to accept

The sins

Which men offer to her

In lieu of a holy dip

As if they are entitled

Why nobody asks a river

If she also feels

It's her duty to nurture

Nature and humankind

When they assume

She flows to offer

Herself to the sea

She could be on a journey

Of self-discovery

So one day she could command

The mighty Ocean to sweep her off feet.

~Shweta Hitesh Joshi

Commentary on Poem 1:

The identity of something that exists is not noticed, but taken for granted. This poem, for me, is as much literal as it is metaphorical. I would go ahead and suggest that the river is analogous to a woman. I will summarize the analogy at the end of this commentary.

Poet Shweta has travelled the thin line of subtle optimism and rhetorical satire. It is also a poem pointing out the wanton and unscrupulous pollution of rivers, expecting the debris to go away into the deep ocean.

Water takes the shape of the bowl it holds. Similarly, the identity of a river is always linked to its **purpose**. Humans started settling down around rivers. Rivers brought water and alluvial soil, two key inputs for an agrarian life.

The societies and civilizations like the Nile, Yellow & Pearl River, Indus, and the Euphrates, have borne civilizations that lasted centuries. These societies have worshipped these rivers as their mothers, life-givers, and deities. In the process of deification, the rivers' existence is taken for granted, and eventually, left as a footnote in the daily lives of those who live off them.

> Why nobody asks a river
> if she gets tired
> of crossing jungles and mountains
> of flowing through bridges and between the cities

The first point to note is the tone of the question. It is the question to the reader, and not to the river itself. The river itself flows along, present at its origin and estuary at the same time, and everywhere in its path at all points in time. So where does she get tired?

It crosses numerous impediments both in the cities (*flowing through bridges and between the cities*) and outside them (*crossing jungles and mountains*), but is it hard work for her? Is the river drowning itself in fatigue? Does the river ever get tired?

A river is a river because it flows. Like how the sun rises and sets. Like how the earth goes round. The purpose of its life is ceaseless activity. What if, a river stops? Why cannot it stop?

> The flowing river
> never stops
> and yet the water

never stays the same.

— *Kamo no Chōmei, Hojoki: Visions of a Torn World*

The intrinsic energy of the river is kinetic. But the point is not about the river's momentum or movement. The point is why nobody asks about the river, even as a matter of courtesy. The answer could be that a river is supposed to flow and it is supposed to be tireless. This rationale is acceptable. Rivers ought to flow and be fresh. But why did it never occur to anybody to ask? Is the flower tired of blooming?

> (Why nobody asks a river)
>
> If she really wants to accept
> the sins
> which men offer to her
> In lieu of a holy dip
> As if he is entitled

Humans! How they take nature for granted!

Apart from being a giver, the river is expected to be an 'absorber' of sin. If one takes a '*holy dip*', the '*sins*' are washed away. That is alright as long as the man does not take this 'service' by the river for granted, but he seems to do so — in the poet's words '*as if he is entitled*'.

As much as the lines bring out the transactional nature of the relationship between humans and rivers, they bring out the attitude of humans towards those transactions. Lack of gratitude is the overwhelming outcome of such entitlement.

> Why nobody asks a river
> if she also feels
> it's her duty to nurture
> Nature and humankind

Rivers, like nature and trees, bless us with their benevolence. They play their part in nature and nurture humankind. We feel entitled because it's available to us without cost from nature, and in this case, rivers. They say anything free is not valued.

> When they assumed
> she flows to offer
> herself to the sea.

Every journey comes to an end. For the river, the inevitable end is to merge with the sea or ocean. This end is portrayed by many poets philosophically. One such portrayal is by Khalil Gibran in his famous poem 'The River Cannot Go Back'.

Let us examine the human point of view brought out by the poet, and juxtapose the deep lines of Gibran.

> It is said that before entering the sea
> a river trembles with fear.

The river goes through myriad emotions like awe, fear, and surrender when it reaches its estuary. A river, to Gibran, is akin to humans that carry emotions and decisions in its heart. On the other hand, humans themselves, according to the poet, expostulate the humanization of rivers — mostly, assuming that rivers draining into the sea is just a natural phenomenon.

There is a reason for me pondering about the merger of the river with the sea. It is the 'death' of the river, yet nobody talks about it that way. Humans think that the river would '*offer*' itself to the sea. The tone here is that of 'submission', according to the poet.

Extending the previous callous attitude of the humans, this thought is an extension of patriarchy, which does not value other segments' values and contributions.

> She could be on a journey
> of self-discovery
> so one day she could command
> the mighty Ocean to be swept off feet

The last stanza of the poem is an expression of revolt, a revolt to break the glass ceiling. A river is **not** for only others, but also for itself. Its life is its own '*journey of self-discovery*'.

Above all, the river may rise from it is position of submissive benevolence, to a dominant position ending up *'sweeping the mighty Ocean off its feet'.*

The poem brings out how 'submissive benevolence' is evolved as a 'purpose for identity' by patriarchal minds. The minds that devalue and denigrate the great contributions of other humans and nature. The metaphorical view of today's feminist battle vs patriarchy is most fitting too.

As we read the poem, we feel guilty about abusing and neglecting one of Nature's great entities and devolving its identity into submissive benevolence. A poem that carries overarching lessons to the humans.

Poem 2: 'I am'

Figure 9 I am' said the Sky …Image by Tobias Hämmer from Pixabay

"I am", said the Sky
   and all the clouds quivered with
   tears of gratitude.

~Elizabeth R Urabe

Commentary on Poem 2:

In the first poem, we saw how nature is designed to be altruistic, yet humans take things for granted. By extension, the construction of a 'natural' entity's identity is based on human perceptions and attitudes.

This poem, 'I am', disavows the views of humans, and focuses on intrinsic views of identity for such natural entities. Here, as Poet Elizabeth Urabe exalts, identity is about confidence.

Confidence comes from self-awareness. Now self-awareness, when created with external motivation (without), is purely relative. But when one looks within, the confidence lights up an internal glow, a radiance that comes from the innermost recesses of our soul. That is absolute.

What more can there be a great example of an identity, that exudes confidence within? The Sky.

The sky is omnipresent. It is the vision of the universe to the naked eye. It is the heavens. It is where the Gods reside. It is endless and eternal, exuding the endlessness of space and time of this universe.

> "I Am", said the Sky

The confident soul which is aware of its inner radiance is enlightened. Let me explain this further.

The inner belief that there is a purpose of existence, and clarity that the purpose is to bring the best out of people — which are their inner radiance and belief — make the words 'I am' not only a factual resonance of existential state but a beacon of hope for those who are yet to discover their purpose of existence, hence their identities.

One may ask why we should quote from the scriptures. In many instances, the seeker of identity has fallen short due to incapacitation of the body or persistence of will, or shortage of a lifetime. The radiance from the blessed soul, sometimes, if not always, helps to cross the bridge in a lifetime. Such an encounter for the seeker of his own identity and purpose and the experience thereof could be dictated by the place and time.

> And all the clouds quivered with
> tears of gratitude.

The radiance of the absolute divine reflects its identity — the sky itself is a reflection of the vast expanse of the universe.

But what about its purpose?

The purpose is always external, and relative. If there is no seeker, there is nothing to be sought. For the sky to radiate its brilliance, the clouds are needed. Here, the clouds are the quintessential seekers.

The '*quivering*' action is essentially the experience of realization of the Gospel truth of the radiance of the absolute divine. (Note the layering of adjectives and pronouns to translate the experience of quivering — that is the power of poetry.)

It is a feeling only a seeker can experience. It is like the 'chill' on one's feet that can only be experienced when one walks among the mounds of the *Cherrapunji* Mountain. It is like a new author touching the first copy of her book.

The '*tears of gratitude*', are the rains that the clouds bring upon the earth below. The bringing of rains is the act of benevolence supporting growth and bountiful abundance. The rains bring life and hope. The rains are the purpose of the clouds' existence.

Now, let us put it all together. There is an absolute divine, whose inner radiance of self-awareness exudes limitless confidence, and such confidence is consumed by the seeker. The seeker, in turn, is titillated, attains the clarity of his / her purpose, and performs an act of benevolence that helps a larger number of beneficiaries.

Identity and Purpose:

As we ruminate on the two elements of our existence — identity and purpose, we also subsume the contrasting approaches by both poets. The complexity of the questions makes the search for answers difficult unless one is a true seeker.

Whether it is the callous attitude of the humans on the river, or it is the shining radiance of the sky that exalts the clouds their purpose, the questions around identity and purpose shall remain for eternity.

I humbly thank Shweta Hitesh Joshi and Elizabeth Urabe for the two great poems. I shall cherish this experience of seeking answers inside the poems for the two great questions of our existence. I will leave this review with a quote.

> "Your duty is to be and not to be this or that. 'I am that I am' sums up the whole truth. The method is summed up in the words 'Be still'. What does stillness mean? It means destroy yourself. Because any form or shape is the cause for trouble. Give up the notion that 'I am so and so'. All that is required to realize the Self is to be still. What can be easier than that?"
> — Ramana Maharshi

~Ashok Subramanian

4. SILENCE

We are back to our nests. COVID19's second wave is ravaging the subcontinent. An apocalyptic scenario indeed. Since I am in India, I am unable to avoid reference to contemporary events that have become contextual to my review. Having said that, poem reviews are where I find my liberation, as you, the reader, might have deduced by now.

I stay still and in silence. I have been led to the point of contemplating the power of the non-spoken word. How? From yogis of the yore to today's seers, poets, and philosophers, the idea of silence and space has been core to human identity and existence.

Space is all-encompassing, comprising both matter and empty elements. Infinite emptiness is the permanent, holistic form of nature. Matter is transient. Emptiness, implying space, is permanent.

Silence is too. From silence is sound born. A blip amid the infinite. A spark amid infinite darkness. A drop of water amid an infinite ocean. Sound causes ripples and ripples cause instability. But silence is permanent. It is the restful form of sound. The beginning, the space between, and the end of the sound.

The spiritual and physical realms of humans have always been connected. Scientists, psychologists, and philosophers alike have agreed on this interposing of both realms.

For us, dear reader, we will fall back on what we love to do most. Explore the world of silence and space, through poems. We get lucky sometimes when we get three poems to churn and cherish.

First is 'Silence', a triplet by Elizabeth Urabe, which explores the purity of silence. The second poem, by Desiree Driesenaar, aptly named 'Folded Silence' is a deep exploration of silence and space, within and without. The third poem, 'Silence, the much-awaited guest' by Sourabha Rao, is about the marriage of silence with darkness, birthing the night. What more can a *'Ponderer'* dream of? I brood in silence, in my own space (literally), about these three poems.

Let me share the three poems and their interweaving of space and silence into the realms of physics, spirituality, and psychology.

Poem 1: Silence

Figure 10 Silence is holy … Image by 4144132 from Pixabay

Silence is holy
and wholly voluminous.
Why taint it with words?
-Elizabeth R Urabe

Commentary on Poem 1:

Elizabeth Urabe is my spiritual connection. No wonder her words are a few, but they open up the space for my exploration.

Humans are born to speak and communicate. Speech is one of

the abilities that make us different from other species. So, why not speak all the time? Speaking is action, communication, and venting, all in one act. So why silence?

Silence, as it turns out, is a figure of speech. It is the absence of the spoken word or sound. In physics, there is no wave, but a flat line.

Let us dissect 'holy' first. Merriam Webster explains holy as 'exalted or worthy of complete devotion as one perfect in goodness and righteousness'. While speech is an act, the poet calls its absence 'holy'. Let me attempt to decipher the phrase *'Silence is holy'*.

Silence is natural and peaceful, reflecting either a state of rest or harmonic motion. When a word is spoken, it is weighed its worth. Such measurement is related to the context, tone, and choice of words. It is relative.

But silence is absolute. It is left to the beholder's interpretation. The unspoken word or the absence of words, called silence, has been spoken. This interpretation is exalted and worthy of complete devotion.

Silence is also *'wholly voluminous'*, says the poet. Wholly voluminous is ever pervading. Imagine infinite space beyond the boundaries of this universe. Silence is the all-occupier of that space. I would bring this out as a psychological and philosophical concept.

One can think only in silence. Even if one has to react in an instant, there is a moment of priority and pause, which is indeed a moment of silence. There are long periods of silence when one 'thinks through' a response. Silence is inevitable for humans to think. Silence is the medium in which one can observe, interpret, process and consume.

Silence is also the gateway to inner discovery. Silence awakens the spirit. The spirit, which is the life of the soul, works its way with the larger universe. The inner conscience speaks but without sound. The conversation within us is silent. This silence is the medium through which the seeker receives his answers. The medium makes the human whole.

Given the glory and holiness of silence, do we need anything more? *'Why taint it with words?'* queries the poet. Words, which I had mentioned before, are always judged and measured. Human judgment is fallacious and contextual.

Silence is absolute. Inner discovery is absolute. Words or noises are undesirable specks of dust that destroy the purity of the silence.

> "God is silent. Now if only man would shut up."
> — Woody Allen

Poet Elizabeth Urabe has captured the magnitude of divinity and infinity succinctly, in a thrifty poem.

Poem 2: Folded Silence

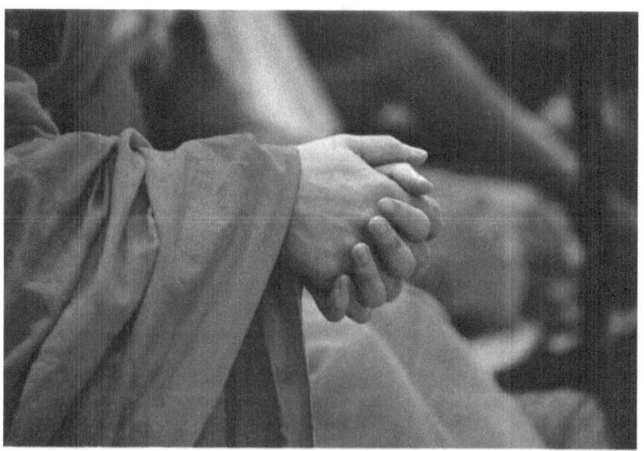

Figure 11 Folded Silence… Image by Pexels from Pixabay

The sound of silence
speaks to me of space
filled with waves
of nothingness.

Or is it nothingness?

*Do we really understand
    the magic of space?*

*Space is between our atoms
    and cells. Space is holding us
    together.*

Silence is space.

*In poems and prose,
    the silence speaks volumes.
    The whiteness is where
    words are becoming
    new meanings.*

*Folded silence,
    folded space,
    becomes
    folded foreverness
    if not opened
    by space.*

*Space is needed
    for new things to emerge.
    Slowing down is needed
    to hear the sound
    of your longing.*

*Unfold, my friends, unfold.
    Only movement, space, and time
    will unleash, emerge, and become*

whatever.

Whatever we long for.
Whatever we want
our lives to be.

Folded silence
wants to be
unfolded.

— Desiree Driesenaar

Commentary on Poem 2:

I had to prepare myself to write this piece. Elizabeth's poem brought to us the 'holiness and wholly voluminous' dimension, akin to space, while Desiree brings us the concept directly, a perfect extension of the first poem.

Does silence have a physical attribute? I never thought about it till I came across this poem by Desiree. Most of us, especially students of science will remember that anything that is visualized is in the context of three dimensions of space and one dimension of time. We will explore the time dimension of silence in Poem 3. Let us explore the space dimension of silence now.

The sound of silence
speaks to me of space
filled with waves
of nothingness.

Or is it nothingness?

Can silence speak? If so, how does it 'sound'? The voice of silence is absolute because it is a *space filled with waves of nothingness*.

Silence is the absence of noise or the spoken word. In that absence, there is meaning though. The meaning of nothing is the start 'before sound', the gap 'between sounds', and the end 'when sound ends'.

Without the start, interval, and end, the sound itself is meaningless. For this reason, the 'nothingness' of sound, that occupies most of the space, defines the very 'essence' of sound.

The attribute through which silence defines sound is 'space'. Space is a three-dimensional medium. It is filled with vacuum and matter. The portion of vacuum is many times over, more than matter. A vacuum is a nothingness.

Now, space is empty. So a 'space of nothingness' is 'nothingness', and vice versa. The poet lets the reader discover this transposition of 'noun' on the 'adjective'.

> Do we really understand
> the magic of space?
>
> Space is between our atoms
> and cells. Space is holding us
> together.
>
> Silence is space.

The next few lines of the poem elaborate on this transposition. We dive into the understanding of 'space'. Now, space, which is fundamental to all our existence, is *magic*. The magic is 'being' — the sheer existence of space, which in turn reflects our existence. Without space, we don't exist. And if we don't exist, we can't realize space. Both space and we are cut from the same cloth.

Even when filled with 'matter', space exists. The poet explains this *'Space is between our atoms and cells. Space is holding us together.'*

The fundamental building blocks of nature — atoms, and cells, occupy space. In between them is space. Space holds us all together. The four forces — strong nuclear, weak nuclear, gravitational, and electromagnetic forces that work alone and together, hold the atoms and cells in place. To act, the forces need space.

Space is the container that holds the matter, and is also contained in the gaps between the fundamental entities that occupy space (the container and contained).

The last line 'Silence *is space*' brings these two concepts together. We had discovered this transposing relationship as 'the start, end and the gaps between matter particles is space' and 'the start, end and the gaps between sounds (read waves) is silence. Silence is therefore the container and contained. If you were to sign up for more physics, then you will discover that space is the material form of silence, and silence is the energy form of space.

Beyond the physical realm, there is a spiritual transference as well. Read this.

> "Space and silence are two aspects of the same thing. The same no-thing. They are externalization of inner space and inner silence, which is stillness: the infinitely creative womb of all existence."
> — Eckhart Tolle, the Power of Now: A Guide to Spiritual Enlightenment

Space and silence are interrelated and are the manifestations of each other — matter and energy. (Einstein must be proud of Desiree Driesenaar here). People dismiss 'nothing', but it is 'nothing' that holds everything (I may sound obtuse here, but this is an attempt to explain the paradox.)

> In poems and prose,
> the silence speaks volumes.
> The whiteness is where
> words are becoming
> new meanings.

With these lines, I feel at home and at peace, as they are about poetry and literature. Let's the spirituality, psychology, and physics fester a bit.

'In poems and prose, the silence speaks volumes.' Indeed. We have just begun to unravel the synonymy of silence and space. We all acknowledge the multi-dimensionality, don't we?

'*The whiteness is where words are becoming new meanings*', explains the poet. Like the proverbial space, a white paper is empty. When you fill it with words and sentences, there are gaps between words, lines, and sentences. Without the gaps, the words won't mean a thing. The written words follow the same meaning as the speech and 'matter' that we saw.

We are now acclimatized to the synonymy, but is there a functional relationship between silence and space? The poet endeavours to bring about the functional aspect in these lines.

> Folded silence
> folded space,
> becomes
> folded foreverness
> if not opened
> by space.
>
> Space is needed
> for new things to emerge.
> Slowing down is needed
> to hear the sound
> of your longing.

It is important to understand '*folded*'. Folded means 'bent over itself' so that one part covers another'. 'Folded' is also a euphemism for 'wrapped and trapped'.

Vast, open spaces create opportunities for genesis and growth. The poet brings the time element into play '*Folded silence, Folded space becomes folded foreverness*', to point that if trapped silence and space aren't freed, they are stuck for eternity, '*if not opened by space.*'

'*This space is needed for new things to emerge*', is about new ideas appearing at the horizon when you are silent and listening. New ideas lead to new deeds. How do we let new ideas and things emerge?

Is silence only the unspoken word? Is silence the calm between, before, or after sound? There is another dimension to silence.

The poet brings this out beautifully, but you can notice only when you are S.I.L.E.N.T. Now L.I.S.T.E.N. The anagram plays up to our wanton interpretation, my friends. By being silent and listening you give space.

> "When I say I love the silence, I'm not being entirely truthful. What I actually love are the abundant, delicate sounds that amplify when I'm silent. These curious creaks, mutters, and hums compel my imagination."
> — Richelle E. Goodrich, Making Wishes: Quotes, Thoughts, & a Little Poetry for Every Day of the Year

If you want to listen, you have to slow down. *'Slowing down is needed to hear the sound of your longing'.* If you move forward without slowing down, you lose silence, space, and ultimately peace. To listen to the *'sound of your longing',*

> Unfold, my friends, unfold.
> Only movement, space, and time
> will unleash, emerge, and become
> whatever.

When one slows down, one unfolds. When one unfolds, one's body, mind, and soul open up. *'Only movement, space, and time will unleash, emerge, and become whatever'.* The concepts of inner engineering, discovery, and evolution happen based on how one slows down and opens up.

> Whatever we long for.
> Whatever we want
> our lives to be.

What would we want or long for? It could be a spiritualistic or materialistic goal. It is in your subconscious mind. Let the desires of your life flower and grow. Build your inner-self, says the poet.

> Folded silence
> wants to be
> unfolded.

The poet finishes emphatically, talking about the need to 'unwrap and release' the 'folds' in the inner recesses of our minds. By *'unfolding'*, there is an open space for us to observe, ponder, assimilate and imbibe, like soil that accepts the seed, the rain, and the shine to produce the magic of sapling.

We leave this poem with a sense of inner solace as if we have discovered our own space, breathing in and out to discover things anew.

Poem 3: Silence, a much-awaited guest

Figure 12Silence as night descends… Image by PublicDomainPictures from Pixabay

Noises fade from the streets as night descends
like voices falling into a whisper while uttering a prom-
ise

~ Sourabha Rao

Commentary on Poem 3:

We have explored the silence within, what about the world? On this fourth planet from the sun, silence happens when the sun sets and ends when the sun rises. This time between sunrise and sunset, which we call 'night', is the temporal spouse of silence. Parallel this with the interpretation that darkness is the photonic counterpart of silence, much like that silence is the auditory counterpart of darkness.

The retraction of noise from the streets by reduced human activity connects with the main focus of the second poem, where silence is the auditory counterpart of space (emptiness). The Night is the temporal counterpart of silence and space, exhorts, poet Sourabha Rao.

> Noises fade from the streets as night descends

Streets are the communion of houses. Houses contain people and people make noises. *'As night descends'*, the humans return to their nests, and the noise recedes.

Body and mind demand quiet. Quiet needs cessation of activities at both physical and mental levels. These active and inactive states are governed by temporal cycles of day and night. The insertion of the temporal dimension is the final piece of the 'silence' puzzle.

> "Q: Why do I love thee, O Night?
> A: Because you know I will never answer."
> — Vera Nazarian

We all love the night for its emptiness, darkness, and silence. Some of us allow our creative and introspective senses to kick in, in the night. There is a world of silence, emptiness, and darkness that lie in front of us to be discovered and explored. Silence is the sound of the night.

> Like voices falling into a whisper while uttering a promise

Have you ever made a promise? Most promises that stick, and are sincere are made in a low voice, whispered, slowly and steadily, with a deep sense of assurance. The strength of the words spoken is absolute, like silence itself.

> "Empty streets are a blessing for you because an empty street
> whips your thoughts and makes you question your life! He who
> wants to dive into his depths, let him wander in the empty

streets!"
— Mehmet Murat ildan

It is easy to see those empty streets bring us to the point of contemplation. Contemplation leads to inner discovery. Inner discovery happens when the streets you walk or when you stay at home, with the silence and emptiness around. The definitiveness of those voices brings about a feeling of safety and solace, as the blanket of silence and darkness wraps the blue planet.

The poem leaves us sitting in our beds, just before slumber time, in a cocoon of solace and comfort.

Contemplating

Silence is multidimensional. We have explored the spatial, temporal, literal, and auditory dimensions in the three poems. Each one hooks on to the other, opening a fundamental understanding of our inner selves and the universe. Such an understanding of silence shall stand in good stead in our journey of life.

> "I felt very still and empty, the way the eye of a tornado must feel, moving dully along in the middle of the surrounding hullaba-loo."
> — Sylvia Plath, The Bell Jar

When we understand silence, we can handle tempests in our life, with our silent and contemplative inner core.

While I researching to write this piece, I came across a 'fourth' dimension of the word 'AUM' or 'OM'. As we have seen, there is that silence at the end of the word which in written form is the white space at the end, and when pronounced, the gap between two repetitions. In these forms, silence completes the mantra itself, as explained in the below quote.

> "Om is said to be a four-syllable word in Sanskrit, originally as AUM. A, th waking state. U, the dream state. M, the unconscious state. And the fourth, the silence that surrounds it — wherefrom everything arises and where to everything inevitably returns.
>
> It is the silence that surrounds Om that contains everything. It is

the silence in your own life that contains and gives birth to everything you have, and everything you will ever need.

It is this same silence we avoid, overlook, and disregard as nothing. The white space of life we abhor. We fill our lives with noise, drama, screens, people, and "stuff" to avoid the void that reminds us of our truth — that beyond flesh that once was not, and will inescapably become not, and we are eternal."
— Drew Gerald

I thank poets Elizabeth Urabe, Desiree Driesenaar, and Sourabha Rao for their wonderful poems that deep dive into multiple dimensions of 'silence'.

~Ashok Subramanian

5. ANXIETY

We are living in hard times. 2020 shocked us. We came out of the year believing that the pandemic was over, but 2021 has brought the pandemic closer to us.

Along with fatalities, casualties, and economic setbacks, the mental health of COVID survivors and the society at large has become a major challenge to deal with. Having seen mental health issues close quarters and still being on it, it is natural for me to explore this topic.

I play Erik Satie's Gnossiennes 1 to 5 in a loop while I write this review. The music flows into my ears, unstringing my nerves and steadying my breath. There is something magical about the piano. It flows into your heart, soul, skin, nerves, and mind, like water. There is no place that it cannot be.

What could be better than exploring the topic I am 'anxious' about than diving into our favorite and familiar methods — reviewing poems. From three different continents — North America, Africa, and Australia, poets Priya Patel, Akinkunmi Akinbode et Adebankemo Oduguwa and Allison Rose Clark bring us anguish and hope in their poems.

Poem 1: Anxiety

Figure 13 Image by agymishel from Pixabay

I am slowly drowning
    The water is so cold and deep
    even the fish
    are scared to swim with me
    I think this is called anxiety
    With arms spread wide
    I float in and out
    on the surface of sanity,
    waiting for the next big wave
    to finally take me away;
    waiting for someone to save me
    In the end, I just keep swimming
    I wonder, for just one moment
    what the quiet would be like;
    the sudden warmth of closing my eyes
    and for just one moment,
    drown myself in tears
    I've never done that before,
    cry I mean, wipe tears away
    with the palm of my hand;
    proof that I too am human
    In the end, I just keep swimming ...

~ Priya

Commentary on Poem 1:

The poem is free-verse and comes with a 5-line construct.

Let us assume that you don't know how to swim and are alone in your boat. Somehow, the boat drifts into deep waters, and suddenly, a wave topples the boat. You are now in the water, deep and dark, without knowing how to swim, the surface is undulating. You are starting to choke...

A poem brings out this 'drowning in the deep ocean' situation — a situation that we face in our daily lives. Problems and situations that we don't know how to handle and in turn that make us anxious — the fear of the depth, the fear of the next wave that might topple us, the desire to live, all combined into one knot, somewhere deep inside us, in our guts... let us dive into the poem now.

> With arms spread wide
> I float in and out
> on the surface of sanity,
> waiting for the next big wave
> to finally take me away;
> waiting for someone to save me

The poet narrates her experience in the first person. The drowning is *'slow'* and the experience is prolonged and traumatic. It is a double whammy for the suffering person.

Fishes are never scared to swim. If the protagonist sees that 'even the fish are scared to swim with her', it is because of her scared mental frame, which sees fear even with the Pisces who live in water.

> "Everything else than sea is a torment to a fish"
> — Rumi

The creatures remain with their expertise — swimming, and at home — at sea as Rumi says, but the protagonist feels that the fish is out of place — scared to swim in the sea! That is re out-of-place feeling. The poet calls it 'anxiety'. So we get it. Anxiety is the out-of-place feeling.

If anxiety was an out-of-place feeling, then how would the protagonist respond? Anxiety paralyzes minds and bodies. The poet illustrates this with a visual. The protagonist *'floats in and out on the surface of sanity'*. There is a world where objectivity and reasoning make sense.

But once you are in 'sinking' mode, you lose this 'common sense' as you are overwhelmed with anxiety. The *'surface of sanity'* is the border between 'anxious insanity' and 'serene sanity'. Floating in and out of this surface is a fringe behaviour that makes the person's actions unreliable.

Now let us look at the physical demeanour. The poet vividly portrays the scene — the protagonist is floating with her *'arms spread wide'* — a gesture of giving up, because her mind is frozen and unreliable, crippled by overwhelming anxiety.

So what is she waiting for? She is waiting for the *'next big wave'*. There is anticipation. The word *'next'* indicates that there is an event in the past, a 'previous' big wave. Therefore, the anxiety, if we appreciate the protagonist's past, stems from a previous event. It goes back to the backstory I had presented at the start of this discourse. The *'big wave'* is a disruptive event, which can put her future in jeopardy.

Stop here for a moment. If you were in that situation, floating with arms wide, and drowning in and out of the deep and cold sea, waiting for the next wave, unsure — anxiety builds — that creepy, knotting feeling inside.

This line *'waiting for someone to save me'* seems to be an afterthought by the poet. It trips the flow of the poem but makes sense if you are holding on to the overall meaning. As one is immersed in their mental wallowing, the thought of 'seeking help' is positive action. Yet, it makes sense, because, it shows the first sign of the protagonist wanting to exit the situation.

The two scenarios are contrasting. On one hand, she waits for the next big way to hit, but on the other hand, she waits for somebody to rescue her. A classical dilemma of the anxious mind!

> In the end, I just keep swimming
> I wonder, for just one moment
> what the quiet would be like;

She keeps herself on the '*surface*', as she still '*keeps swimming*'. Her thoughts wander back to the fringe of sanity. Somewhere, '*for just one moment*', the protagonist wonders '*what the quiet would be like*'. Quietness, to the tumultuous mind, is a dream.

> "Quiet is peace. Tranquility. Quiet is turning down the volume knob on life. Silence is pushing the off button. Shutting it down. All of it. — Amir"
> — Khaled Hosseini, The Kite Runner

That is a wish, a dream. And that dream — the wish for quietness — comes and goes in the protagonist's mind in the blip of a second.

> The sudden warmth of closing my eyes
> and for just one moment,
> drown myself in tears
> I've never done that before,
> cry I mean...

The dream is trapped in the 'closing my eyes', says the protagonist. Once the eyes are closed, the actual quiet moment is born. The '*quiet*' that was a wish before, now becomes real. 'Just *for one moment*', again.

She '*drowns herself in tears*'; Note the difference between the external situation of drowning in her situation — mentioned in the opening lines, and the internal letting goes, '*drowning in tears*'. The first part is beyond the protagonist's control, the second one — the crying—is about taking control.

'*I've has never done that before*', she admits. So far, she had been waiting for the big wave to consume or someone to save her but when she spent 'one moment' thinking about the quiet, she let go, and from her closed eyes, *'warm tears'* flowed. She *'cries'*.

> Wipe tears away
> with the palm of my hand;
> proof that I too am human
> In the end, I just keep swimming ...

As the protagonist *'wipes tears away with the palm of her hand, crying proves that she too is human.'* Indeed. Crying makes us vulnerable, and vulnerability makes us human.

> "Do not apologize for crying. Without this emotion, we are only robots."
> — Elizabeth Gilbert, Eat, Pray, Love

At some point time, crying is about letting go. Beyond that, a decision has to be made to act. The act is — to *'just keep swimming'*. So if you realize that when anxiety paralyzes the mind, at some point, 'acceptance' and 'letting go' set in, and action is inevitable. The inner quiet is the ultimate panacea for the anxious protagonist.

> "Crying is all right in its way while it lasts. But you have to stop sooner or later, and then you still have to decide what to do."
> — C.S. Lewis, The Silver Chair

The poem leaves us with a mixed feeling — the natural anguish of the situation and the inevitability of dealing with it.

Poem 2: Rare Escapade

Laced with turbulence deep in the blue,
People flourished sailing on,
But the fear is...onlookers don't feel the waves...
Until we mastered to prevail,
We move!

Oceans winks; anxiety flipped
the risk was sweet
A class with zeal that dares the freeze
we smile like time to come
an epic moment for our fear to succumb.

The grieved and the oppressed
the morning dew and the sunset
the season and its affairs
A clue to a pleasant mind-set

Our heads bow,
The boat yet moved,
Her mind skipped,
My head hurt,
In all, all we had is us and we can't feed the beasts
with none.

> *We must move to the satisfying shore.*

> *~Akinkunmi Akinbode et Adebankemo Oduguwa*

Commentary on Poem 2:

Each one of us is born with a gift. This gift is hidden somewhere, like a gem in the womb of the sea. The purpose of our lives is to find out this hidden gem, polish it, and present it to the world. But this is not an easy matter.

Somehow, in our minds, we have thoughts that hold us back. Poets **Akinkunmi Akinbode** et **Adebankemo Oduguwa** bring out the mental blocks, the anxiety, and the final solution in bringing out the opportunity. Here in their own words-

> The summary of the poem is actually what you go through in life's adventure... We are so much afraid of the unknown but the resources available to scale through shouldn't be the determining factor to getting to the peak of your success... ~Akinkunmi

The *'fear of the unknown'* creates anxiety, and the challenge is within than without.

> Laced with turbulence deep in the blue,
> People flourished sailing on,

'Deep in the blue', brings back the same memories as Poem 1. The *'deep blue'*, metaphorically represents life. *'Laced with turbulence'*, is the deep blue — that is, troubles in life. The poets acknowledge the challenges in life.

People have succeeded in the past. Millions lived their lives before us. There are those mighty examples of the past. The *'people flourished sailing on'*, indicates that deep blue has been conquered before.

> But the fear is...onlookers don't feel the waves...
> Until we mastered to prevail,
> we move!

The 'flourishing' in the past did not happen without effort. It happened because '*we mastered to prevail*' (practice) and we '*moved*' (action). A journey across the deep blue comes through 'practice', and 'action'.

But when one stands on the shore and looks at the sea, there is that fear — the fear of the unknown enters the mind. '*Onlookers don't feel the waves*', so they are daunted and awed by the magnitude of the deep blue before them.

The tentative human stands at the edge of the water and dips his toe in the foam. When a wave comes toward them, they step back. They don't get wet. Their minds are comfortable when their feet are in *terra firma*. That is the fear of the unknown. For those who practice and act, this fear is non-existence. This fear of the unknown is **anxiety.** It is this anxiety that separates the onlookers from the masters.

> Oceans winks; anxiety flipped
> the risk was sweet
> A class with zeal that dares the freeze
> we smile like time to come
> an epic moment for our fear to succumb.

Maybe, the onlookers overthought. Maybe, their minds were overwrought. They were scared to take the plunge. They scare — the fear that held them back — the anxiety, is the one that was pushing them to the edge. Anxiety is always a fence sitter.

> "It's OKAY to be scared. Being scared means you're about to do something really, really brave."
> — Mandy Hale, The Single Woman: Life, Love, and a Dash of Sass

Did we say that the poets were serious, especially about anxiety? Nope. There is that subtlety of humour that comes out — 'the *ocean winks*'. It says 'come to me, take the plunge, and master me'. The invite is too tempting, the fence-sitter takes the plunge –'*the anxiety flips*'. The temptation, the lure, the attraction — is too much to ignore. 'The *risk was sweet*', wasn't it? Indeed, the plunge is taken!

The momentum created by the *'risk taking'*, which *'flipped the anxiety'* is sustained by a *'class with zeal'*, say the poets. The class has attributed to the mastery that brings the flourish, as we have seen earlier. This brings us to zeal.

Zeal is the spring of curiosity and enthusiasm that challenges the remnants of anxiety or uncertainty if any that might have lingered in the corners. The zeal *'dares the freeze'*; the freeze here is the mental inertia.

> "Saw a little girl touch a big bug and shout, "I conquered my fear! YES!" and calmly walk away. I was inspired."
> — Nathan Fillion

The 'zeal', 'practice', and 'action' that we have seen so far have cleared the cobwebs of anxiety in the minds of the 'master'. So *'we smile like time to come'* — a smile of confidence and a certain future (*'time to come'*). That *moment* is *'epic'*, as it is the 'point in time for the fear to succumb', obliterated by the confidence gained?

> The grieved and the oppressed
> the morning dew and the sunset
> the season and its affairs
> A clue to a pleasant mind-set

We have seen that the evolution from the 'onlooker' to the 'master' is a combination of zeal, risk-taking, practice, and action. All these factors have evolved from within. The poets help us take a look around though. The external factors — *'the grieved and the oppressed'* — indicating the state of people, the time of day — *'the morning dew and the sunset'*, the weather and time of year — *'the season and its affairs'*, are enjoyed by a person who has a still mind and has overcome anxiety and the internal tumult. The poet unveils this with *'a clue to the pleasant mind set'*.

> Our heads bow,
> The boat yet moved,
> Her mind skipped,
> My head hurt,

In all, all we had is us and we can't feed the beasts with none.
We must move to the satisfying shore.

'*The boat yet moved*', it could be in the deep blue sea, or from the shore to sea. It reflects a state of progress. It requires an effort, in such an effort '*our heads bow(ed)*'. You might notice a bit of first-person here. Both poets are about to go on a voyage.

The effort to master takes its toll. '*Her mind skipped, my head hurt*' might indicate the effort to cope. The poets reconcile to their situation — accept it (all *we had is us and we can't feed the beasts with none*). The poets, while acknowledging the struggles, risks, and rewards of the voyage in the deep blue, eventually, have to reach the 'satisfying shore'. The shore here is a destination, a milestone — which is driven by a sense of accomplishment and satisfaction. Overcoming the anxiety would be worth it if the goal is reached.

The poem brings about a multidimensional view of the 'journey of anxiety'. Kudos to the poets for providing an in-depth experience.

Poem 3: Panixious Plea

Figure 14 Image by Claudio_Scott from Pixabay

Calm my anxious
    Spirit.
    Still my racing
    Thoughts.
    Give me peace
    within my heart.
    Make worry
    Take a stroll.
    Let desperation
    Drift away
    like currents
    Carry water.
    Relax my body
    and my mind.
    Some things
    I can't control.

   ~Allison Rose Clark

Commentary on Poem 3:
While the first two poems bring out the experiences that people undergo through anxiety, the third poem, 'Panixious Plea' by Allison Rose Clark, written in 2014, brings out a beautiful recipe for handling anxiety. Anxiety is a physical response to the 'unknown.' The prescription is simple yet profound. It is so simple that the reader may feel anticlimactic. But after going through 'hell', it is worthwhile to sit and read the recipe. The world needs healers, and healing starts with self.

    Calm my anxious
    Spirit.
    Still my racing
    Thoughts.

A simple start to the poem brings out the situation and the response. 'Anxious spirit' induced by 'racing thoughts', is the situation. The mind that is the monkey, is jumping from one branch to another, as new thoughts stemming from anxiety race across the feeble mind. Anxiety is from the core here — from the spirit. The poet implores us not to react, but respond. Respond with calm, and being still. Such a measure response makes us the observer of the anxiety and thoughts that stem from it, but also the muster a calm response.

> Give me peace
> within my heart.
> Make worry
> Take a stroll.

I love these lines *'Give me peace within my heart'*. **Inner peace**. The costliest thing a human can possess. Peace within my heart. The peace that settles in the place where emotions are born. It is like dumping a glacier into a volcano spewing lava. The fizz around the collision is undeniable, but what happens after, is infinite calm. The ability to take things as they are, and not to heart — **acceptance** — is the key to inner peace.

> "Anxiety was born in the very same moment as mankind. And since we will never be able to master it, we will have to learn to live with it — just as we have learned to live with storms."
> — Paulo Coelho, Manuscrito encontrado em Accra

We cannot wish away anxiety. Anxiety is a natural phenomenon, but humans can will it to go away. *'Make worry take a stroll.'* A calm, almost yogic response.

> Let desperation
> Drift away
> like currents
> Carry water.

Anxiety leads to desperation. Desperation leads to impetuous actions — actions of last resort. It deprives humans of their biggest strength — rational thinking. The poet exhorts us to the desperation drift away.

Currents in water — ocean or river, are not visible, they move underneath. They determine the direction of water flow and hence many geological and biological events that ensue. The 'drifting away of desperation' is not a superficial process. It is an event inside a human being, and water, the elixir also works to clean the messy leftovers of anxiety. The analogy is more than a coincidence.

> Relax my body
> and my mind.
> Some things
> I can't control.

Finally, the prescription to deal with anxiety is out. 'Relax *my body and my mind*'. The words impound the essence and capture the crux of the entire poem. Many of us may scoff at the simplicity, but in simplicity lies the solution.

So what is the secret sauce? **Acceptance.** Anxiety blinds us to the fact that there are some things in our lives that we cannot control. But once we accept that, it is the first big step in relaxing our minds.

> "For after all, the best thing one can do when it is raining is let it rain."
> — Henry Wadsworth Longfellow

For achieving acceptance, it is about letting go. Let things happen, evolve. Things that happen will happen. Anxiety is a burden that we carry today of what MIGHT happen tomorrow. The poet just simplifies this profound message in this simple line -'*Something I can't control.*'

Soup for the Soul:

The three poems provide warm soup for the anxious soul. Life is about living, and worrying takes away the beauty of life. Anxiety is a natural response — a fear of the unknown and uncertainty of the future. Yet, it can be overcome. The recipes lie in the poems.

As much as we savour the soup, we shall let the learnings percolate into your soul — 'acceptance', 'zeal', 'practice', 'action', 'risk taking', 'seeking the quiet' — all contribute to the liberation of our minds from anxiety.

This was one of my more challenging reviews and caused some anxiety. But as I learned to listen, engage and write, the anxiety about writing this review vaporized. That is my own experience.

~ Ashok Subramanian

6.   THE LITTLE THINGS

The little child inside me wishes to jump out — hop from my mind and be himself. He wants to look and appreciate the little things, yearning for simplicity in this make-do sophisticated lives of adults. I remember the poem by Cecil Frances Alexander that brings out the quest for simplicity and enjoying little things so well.

> All things bright and beautiful,
> All creatures great and small,
> All things wise and wonderful,
> The Lord God made them all.

The poem goes on to describe how beautiful those little things are. So what is so special about little things?

> "Dust is the parent of a star!"
> — Munia Khan

Little things, enjoyed, done, or dealt with, bring action, outcome, accomplishment, and joy. These little things make us see life in the proportion that we can consume and respond to. Savor and enjoy. Dream and do. It is the little acorn that creates a forest. It is the little match that sparks the forest fire. It is the dust that makes the star.

The poems penned by poets Shweta Hitesh Joshi and Deepshikha Shekhawat that we are going to savour today bring out the same essence of simplicity and the joy of little things in their inimitable style.

Poem 1: 'Perhaps'

Figure 15 Perhaps... Happiness has a seraphic connection...
Image by Prawny from Pixabay

Perhaps

Happiness has a seraphic connection

With the soul

And we didn't know yet

Perhaps, what we are chasing is transient

And what we needed was always present

Little did we pause to notice?

The tweets of the birds

And buzz of the bees

The dew on the twigs

Perhaps, we slipped, the shiver of the flower

And the heedless laughter of the river

It was always where it now is

Perhaps we never met the happy-within

~ Shweta Hitesh Joshi

Commentary on Poem 1:

'Perhaps' is a poignant poem that brings out the simple things we miss. The poet's lovely articulation of poignancy by the use of the word 'perhaps' hangs on through the poem. 'Perhaps', according to the Merriam-Webster dictionary means 'used to express uncertainty or possibility'. I can always feel a sigh behind the word, especially when I read this poem.

> Perhaps

> Happiness has a seraphic connection

> With the soul

Have you noticed when you buy toys for your kid or your pet, they ignore and go for the old cardboard box or broken utensil? Have you noticed how they derive joy out of those little things? The instant connection of happiness with simple things is because *'perhaps'*, there is a *'seraphic connection to the soul'*.

Our soul is our eternal identity. It is the naked representation of each human. To make a connection with the soul, the feeling should be authentic, without any decoration. Happiness is one such feeling. If that is the case, *perhaps*, it is easy for us to understand that the child or the pet identifies a simple thing as its source of joy. Such a feeling is pure, simple, and authentic. Hence, the 'seraphic connection to the soul'.

And we didn't know yet

Perhaps, what we are chasing is transient

And what we needed was always present

It is fact. Many among us don't understand that 'happiness' is not a derivative of things that we chase — '*What we are chasing in transient*'. Transience is both illusionary and beautiful. What are we chasing? We are chasing happiness. Happiness is a state of mind, they say. If we think we are happy because we have attended something, then such joy is transient.

So where do we find happiness? The poet is leading us, but not sure, with a qualifying 'perhaps'. Let us follow her lead. '*What we needed was always present*' — the 'happiness' was always around. Around? Present? Where? Why can't we see? '*We didn't know yet*' — Ah! So it is a treasure hunt then. Is the poet messing with us?

Little did we pause to notice?

The tweets of the birds

And buzz of the bees

The dew on the twigs

We did not search enough. What was the need to get frantic? What is the rush for? Have we noticed, when we are driving, that we cannot see the things that whizz past us, like the trees? Our eyes are on the road, we may argue. But if life was a journey and you were the driver, then you are in the fast lane. Too fast that we don't watch the journey, but keep our eyes on some materialistic destination. 'Little did we pause to notice', answers the poet. We can see the 'simple things' only when we take a pause. Take it all in, slow down.

What are we missing in the journey of life? Simple things. They are the '*tweets of the birds*', the '*buzz of the bees*', and the '*dew of the twigs*'. Such things, simple yet magical, are out there. All we had to do was to pause to savour.

> Perhaps, we slipped, the shiver of the flower

> And the heedless laughter of the river

If we pause long enough, 'perhaps', 'perhaps', we can enjoy '*the shiver of the flower*' and '*the heedless laughter of the river*'. But we did not. Note the poignancy that seeps out of the word 'perhaps' here.

> "The world is full of magic things, patiently waiting for our senses to grow sharper."
> — W.B. Yeats

A life, slow and slow enough, to search and savour, reflect and wonder brings more peace and happiness, from the little things around us. We are the ones that need to grow.

> It was always where it now is

> Perhaps we never met the happy-within

The little things are the objects that make us happy. But where and when does happiness happen?

'*It was always where it now is*' — the answer is 'now'. Happiness is experienced now. Once we open our minds and slow down, we will see the simple things, and feel happiness. We don't need to wait or search for our memories. It is there for us to pick and feel right now.

So where does happiness happen? '*We never met the happy-within*', says the poet. Happiness is within us.

The tone of this review is present and hopeful, while the poet has kept the poignancy through. The difference is deliberate, yet the reader shall note that in the regrets lie the lessons. The poet is always right.

Poem 2: 'Little Boy Tim'

Figure 16 Little Boy Tim… Image by Jean Downs from Pixabay

The last evening I met this little boy,
   Playing by himself with enormous joy.
   His eyes were bright and blue,
   Like a sapphire shining in the oceans of glue.
   It seems, his playmates were pebbles and greens,
   Hopping in the mud puddle wearing torn jeans.
   I walk towards the garden to play with him,
   He greeted me with a sweet smile, I nicknamed him Tim.
   He narrated the tales of spirits to me
   while swinging down on the hanging tree.
   Tim gets so much fun out of plants, puppies, and butterflies,
   To my every question he always had in hand replies.
   We ran to his house to take the bicycles out,
   I kept listening while riding, to what he was talking

about.
He shared his passion for becoming a chef,

Got inspiration from his uncle Jeff.
George and Richard are his brothers,
they all love the festival of colours.
He loves going out to the market with his dad,
His favourite snacks are brownies and cheese bread.
He then pleasingly asked me to be his mate,
I accepted his proposal without any wait.
We stopped near a pond and relaxed there for a while,
we both cheered up to the beautiful evening with a smile.

"It was all ended so happily,
awaiting to meet the little boy Tim eagerly!"

~ Deepshikha Shekhawat

Commentary on Poem 2:

This poem by poet Deepshikha Shekhawat is about a little girl meeting a little boy, who enjoyed the little things and then became a happy friend. The poem is narrated in the first person as a tale of simple things, written in rhymes.

Can a little boy find happiness in little things? Let us explore.

> The last evening I met this little boy,
> Playing by himself with enormous joy.
> His eyes were bright and blue,
> Like a sapphire shining in the oceans of glue.

The story is young. Last evening, our narrator (a little girl) met this boy. The boy is happy, *'playing by himself with enormous joy'*. The opening is alluring. The boy was 'happy' — 'happy within'. It is the *seraphic* connection that we saw in the earlier poem.

"Fall
in love
with your solitude"
— Rupi Kaur, Milk and Honey

The boy is happy within and loves his own company. And that's showing. His eyes are *'bright and blue'* — that the colour choice is more reflective than deliberate, and the inherent message is the happiness within. The blue eyes now are also considered figuratively like *'the shining sapphire'*.

> It seems, his playmates were pebbles and greens,
> Hopping in the mud puddle wearing torn jeans.
> I walk towards the garden to play with him,
> He greeted me with a sweet smile, I nicknamed him Tim.

As he plays with himself alone, his friends are *'pebbles and greens'*. It goes back to our original idea of intrinsic happiness. Pebbles and green are found out there, and the little boy knows how to relate to those simple things of joy.

In this stanza, our girl connects with the boy. She is welcomed with a *'sweet smile'*. The intrinsic happiness radiates as a smile. The happy, solitary boy gets a name — Tim. A sweet little imagination by the poet.

> He narrated the tales of spirits to me
> while swinging down on the hanging tree.
> Tim gets so much fun out of plants, puppies, and butterflies,
> To my every question he always had in hand replies.
> We ran to his house to take the bicycles out,
> I kept listening while riding, to what he was talking about.

Tim (now that we have a name) is an adventurous boy. We can picture him in a garden and a neighbourhood. I am sure that Tim and the poet don't belong to this gadget era. A beautiful friendship develops.

'Little things' again come to the fore. The poet in this stanza brings us further into what we may have just gone past, and yet don't want to let go of--our childhood.

> "Everything is ceremony in the wild garden of childhood."
> — Pablo Neruda

Tim *'swings down on the hanging tree'* and he *'gets so much fun out of plants, puppies, and butterflies'*. The active boy blends with nature and draws out fun. His childhood is what we all have heard and yearn for. A sunny neighbourhood. Butterflies and puppies. Plants and trees. And the whole day in front of us children. Sigh. Those days!

The poet also moves the story forward. Tim and the poet, now friends, are in chatty mode. Tim narrates *'tales of spirits'*, he has *'in hand replies'* for her questions. As they go on a bicycle ride together, she is *'listening to what he is talking about'*. We can picture the poet as a listener and Tim, as a witty and wise friend. Conversations strengthen friendship, especially in childhood. With tales, curious questions and know-it-all answers, the children's friendship emerges as a world of its own.

> He shared his passion for becoming a chef,
>
> Got inspiration from his uncle Jeff.
> George and Richard are his brothers,
> They all love the festival of colours.
> He loves going out to the market with his dad,
> His favourite snacks are brownies and cheese bread.

The beautiful conversation grows. Tim shares his identity and life with our girl. He talks about his siblings, uncles, and dad. They all love colours. He talks about his visit to the market and the food he likes.

> "We're all stories, in the end."
> — Steven Moffat

Most conversations about people start with their stories. Stories are those little things that trigger memories in the narrator and moments in the listener. Tim's story enthrals our girl.

> He then pleasingly asked me to be his mate,
> I accepted his proposal without any wait.
> We stopped near a pond and relaxed there for a while,
> We both cheered up to the beautiful evening with a smile.

Finally, Tim asks our girl to be his 'mate, pleasingly'. Again, a little gesture and tone. The enthralled narrator jumps at it — without any wait.' A friendship that is built on little things, she must be feeling. His love for little things, his intrinsic happiness, his stories, and his pleasing gesture — all make him a person to be with.

> "I think you're a fairy tale. I think you're magical and brave, and exquisite. And I hope you'll let me be in your story."
> — Laini Taylor, Strange the Dreamer

That's how our narrator girl must be feeling. 'Let me be part of your fairy tale'. They enjoy the evening together near a pond.

The poem brings out how little things bring happiness and friendship, and how little children build their lives around them. A fresh feel to my reviews.

Those Little Things:

Don't we all long for happiness? Our happiness as children has been robbed by adulthood and its fallacies. The truth is that in children, happiness is pure and simple. That is why little things give them pleasure and happiness.

> "Children are the closest we have to wisdom, and they become adults the moment that final drop of everything mysterious is strained from them."
> — Simon Van Booy, Love Begins in Winter: Five Stories

That, my friend, is what I call wisdom. Wisdom lies in being simple. The poet brings out timeless wisdom by bringing out how children, happiness, and little things are so interconnected. No amount of adulthood can undo this wisdom. For it is the adults who fight wars, and it is the children who love — love simple things.

"And when all the wars are over, a butterfly will still be beautiful."
— Ruskin Bond, Scenes from a Writer's Life

~Ashok Subramanian

7. CONVERSATIONS WITH A CHILD

I love talking to children. Do you?

I always wonder how intelligent can be innocent. Learn it from the children. They can laugh and be happy at nothing — a quality that adults miss. The carefree innocence leads to abundance. We embrace anxiety and guilt when we grow, and lose the carefree innocence.

The conversations with children are a discovery of this abundance and innocence. Yet children also need words of nourishment from us.

> "The soul is healed by being with children."
> — Fyodor Dostoevsky

The words of Dostoevsky ring true, corroborated by the fact that the poets who write about children feel the same. Poetry about children is about learning from them, as much as understanding ourselves. We can converse with children as children and as adults. The first poem, 'Young Homie' by Poet Yasmin Aden, is an exhortation of righteousness by an adult (the poet) and the second, 'Tell you a secret' by Poet Ken Hume, is a small episode of honey and whispers between a father and his daughter. Contrasting as they are, the poems capture the moments of interaction between the parent and the child.

Let us dive right in!

Poem 1: 'Young Homie'

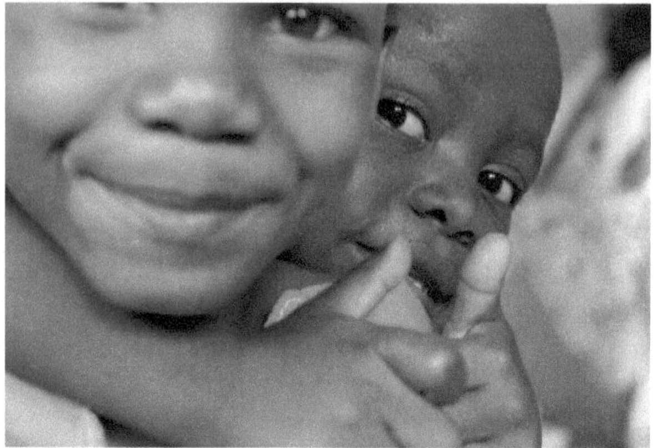

Figure 17 Young Homie... Image by dark-eyed from Pixabay

Look around

And account aloud

Shoes without shoelace

Yet you stand out

Embrace the phase

Please wait

Tie your shoelace

Appreciate with less complain

A child barefoot with the widest

Brightest silent smile

Seen a mile away reconciles

For a while less vocal and noble

Yet struggles but humble

Hold up young homie

Split it ain't about the fast life

Strife and stride

Educate yourself emulate

Hold up young homie

Only uphold for the right cause

For society robs

~Yasmin Aden

Commentary on Poem 1:

The poem is a conversation with a child, yet a discourse on a righteous life. The dual tone of this poem is not obvious, but as we cruise along with the verses we shall discover.

The poem is about the elder talking to a 'young homie'.

> Look around
>
> And account aloud
>
> Shoes without shoelace

You can feel the duality right away. '*Shoe without shoelace*' indicates the carefree nature of the child. Alternately, it could also mean that the child's dilapidated condition, especially coming from an impoverished neighbourhood. But a carefree, impoverished *'homie'* is who the poet is talking to.

Now if the young homie looks around, he can see his adverse circumstances. Let us define *'homie'* now.

> Homie — /'həʊmi/
>
> Noun, INFORMAL·US — an acquaintance from one's town or neighborhood, or a member of one's peer group or gang.

The word 'Homie' is an interesting choice. It brings a community and a neighborhood to the fore, and in turn, sets the context for the poem. The child is a product, and at the same time, the most fertile symbol of a community. The poet brings attention to the child and *'looks around'* and *'accounts aloud'* to awaken the child's senses of his surroundings.

> Yet you stand out
>
> Embrace the phase
>
> Please wait
>
> Tie your shoelace

The young homie's response to the situation he had gathered while *'looking around'* is to now 'stand out', which his ultimate goal is. But how should he start?

'Please wait', the poet exhorts, and advises the homie to *'tie his shoelace'*. The tying of the shoelace is indeed about the preparation before the journey — situational awareness and preparedness, all in simple words, by the poet.

> Appreciate with less complaint
>
> A child barefoot with the widest
>
> Brightest silent smile

Seen a mile away reconciles

For a while less vocal and noble

Yet struggles but humble

The elements of a balanced, prepared and confident path lie ahead of the homie, according to the poet. '*A shoe without a shoe-lace*' is still a covered toe than a '*barefoot*' if only the homie '*appreciates and complains less*'.

The acceptance that the homie is in an impoverished condition is a step-up from the situation awareness, which we saw earlier. Acceptance bequeaths *humility* and *nobility*. Acceptance brings in a reconciliation, even if it is *for a while*. Acceptance brings 'a *silent smile*' despite the struggles. A profound input to the homie, indeed.

> "Nothing brings down walls as surely as acceptance."
> — Deepak Chopra, The Third Jesus: The Christ We Cannot Ignore

For the homie, the acceptance could be difficult and against popular notions. It requires an effort. It is against instinct and popular advice. The poet, however, keeps good counsel.

Hold up young homie

Split it ain't about the fast life

Strife and stride

Educate yourself emulate

The struggle can take a toll, hence the young homie must '*hold up*'. It takes time to build a life through such struggles. Awareness to acceptance, acceptance to action. Action is not about the '*fast life*', but dealing with '*strife*' and '*striding*' over it, and focusing on '*educating oneself*'.

> "Whatever you do will be insignificant, but it is very important

that you do it."
— Mahatma Gandhi

The action that the poet describes to the homie is to build his competence and endurance. Now, there is a purpose for that action. The purpose for that action comes from the heart.

Hold up young homie

Only uphold for the right cause

For society robs

'The society', the poet says, remorseless jungle for survival. Society, especially the young homie's neighborhood can pull one down, and rob them of success. The heartaches for justice — to *'uphold the right cause'*. The action that comes from the heart, is altruistic, putting others above oneself.

"Justice will not be served until those who are unaffected are as outraged as those who are."
— Benjamin Franklin

The poem offers simple, yet beautifully structured advice for the young homie. **Awareness, acceptance, action, and altruism** are four significant elements that will make the young homie a positive contributor in this turbulent world.

Poem 2: 'Tell you a secret'

Somewhere else, while we were reading about the 'Young Homie', a cute interlocution between a father and a daughter — 'Tell you a Secret' by Ken Hume.

Figure 18 Tell you a secret… Image by StockSnap from Pixabay

She ventures over to me slowly
    with a coy expression on her face
    and shuffles up beside me on the couch
    "I want to tell you a secret daddy."
    Her gentle voice utters so quietly
    That I can barely hear.
    "What's that darling?"
    "Daddy, I want to tell you a secret"
    A little louder this time
    yet still with a soft tone.
    Tugging at my arm
    So I decide to play along
    With her game
    Curiosity piqued
    I stoop down real close
    Asking her
    "What do you want to tell me?"
    And so,
    She whispers in my ear
    "Daddy. I want...."
    With a pause for effect
    "I want....

I wait with bated breath

" I want crisps"
Crisps?!
I said to myself.
What an anti-climax!
I chuckle out loud
"Is that it?"
I inquire.
"Yes daddy"
Her mischievous smile
stretching across her face
I push myself up
Venture over to the press
where she's already opened the door
and take out a packet
of 'monster Crips'
as she calls it.
Such cuteness
and brazenness
all in one!

"You're going to turn into a packet of crisps
you know that?!"
I say.
Laughing now.
"No, daddy"
She twisted her head back
laughing in return.
And off she skips
back into the sitting room
having secured her prize.
Sure, how could I resist?

~Ken Hume

Commentary on Poem 2:

This poem drips with innocent, cosy, daddy-love. I don't have a daughter, yet I dote on my nieces. The poem changes my mood to all the good things in this world, yet held inside a cocoon. I can imagine reading this poem on a cold, dark evening, yet inside a home, the father and daughter duo, having a cosy, warm conversation.

> She ventures over to me slowly
> with a coy expression on her face
> and shuffles up beside me on the couch

The warm house adorns a couch. The father is on the couch, the girl approaches the father. Father is her superhero and first love. A love that is pure and innocent, wrapped in safety and warmth.

The '*coyness*' that she expresses, while she '*ventures slowly*', and then '*shuffles up*' beside the father '*on the couch*' — there is the unbridled, innocent excitement oozing out as she approaches her father to share her secret.

> "I want to tell you a secret daddy."
> Her gentle voice utters so quietly
> that I can barely hear.
> "What's that darling?"
> "Daddy, I want to tell you a secret"
> A little louder this time
> yet still with a soft tone.

A gentle voice — '*her gentle voice*', full of innocence and excitement, permeates the air of love. Still, the words are hushed, and the father can barely hear. She intends to tell a secret to her '*daddy*', her confidante. The first is the tone and the second is the matter. The tone is '*gentle and quiet*' the first time, and '*louder yet soft*' the second time. Is it not a blessing for the father, to be called and whispered to, by his dear, darling daughter?

> "Blessed indeed is the man who hears many gentle voices call
> him father."
> — Lydia Maria Child

Then, of course, the matter that is to be kept secret, even when nobody is around. The matter is a secret, and at this stage, I cannot reveal it. The daughter expresses her intent to share a secret, a secret that can be only between them.

> "I want to be with those who know secret things or else alone."
> — Rainer Maria Rilke

The father is the confidante and the girl is the whisperer. The secrets are those little things that strengthen their bond. Let us explore the 'matter' now.

> Tugging at my arm
> So I decide to play along
> With her game
> Curiosity piqued
> I stoop down real close
> Asking her
> "What do you want to tell me?"
> And so,
> She whispers in my ear
> "Daddy. I want...."
> With a pause for effect
> "I want....

The daughter's act of enticing her father, *'piquing'* his *'curiosity'* continues. For the father, the antics of the apple of his eye draw him to the secret. He decides to *'play along with her game'*. Now, the act of delivering a secret commences.

He asks her about the secret. He is curious. He leans close to her and asks. This act of a father is all-encompassing, in particular, a playmate, that the girl can trust. This is a game but played with a person who is trusted completely. Girls have their little secrets, and they can be shared with a person who they trust most — Fathers. Fathers are the epitome of unconditional love and companionship to their daughters.

> "A father is the template of a man Nature gives a girl"
> — Allison Pearson, I Don't Know How She Does It

In this playmate role, the father pops the inevitable question — *"What do you want to tell me?"* The suspense, slow yet *'piquing curiosity'*, plays out now. The girl, whispers the secret... or not yet...in a hushed tone, *'pausing for effect'*, says 'I *want... Daddy, I want...'*

This dramatic effect of the whisper is like the breeze caressing the leaves of a tree, the leaves know they can only dance in the whisper — the father himself, now drawn into the web of the sweet conspiracy that the young girl has laid out. Let us see how the secret plays out.

> I wait with bated breath
>
> " I want crisps"
> Crisps?!
> I said to myself.
> What an anti-climax!
> I chuckle out loud
> "Is that it?"
> I inquire.
> "Yes daddy"
> Her mischievous smile
> stretching across her face

The girl breaks the secret. She *'wants crisps'.* For the besotted father, who was drawn into the web of conspiracy, he was expecting a bombshell. Crisps, just crumbled into an anti-climax before him. Ouch!

> My idea of a meal, if I was hungry, was to open a bag of potato chips. -Sandra Cisneros

His dear daughter has a weakness for crisps. Crisps are her favourite stuff, and she wants them, and that is the big secret! The father, like a lovelorn leaf in the ocean of this deeply hushed conspiracy, is hit with a mild soft wave in hushed tones. It was all about 'crisps'.

Being the loving father he is, he keeps the ball in the game. *'Is that it?'* he inquires, going with the flow. His darling daughter is still at it, 'Yes, daddy', she smiles, like the billion stars twinkling in the sky. And who would not fall for it?

> I push myself up
> Venture over to the press
> where she's already opened the door
> and take out a packet
> of 'monster crisps'
> As she calls it.
> Such cuteness
> and brazenness
> all in one!

It is a race to the press… I would read it on the counter or shelf, or perhaps the fridge. The crisps are there, alright. She has beaten her father to it, *'taking out a packet of 'monster crisps''.* From a cute conspiracy, it became an adorable race, which is won well and truly by the daughter. The father relishes these endearing moments, *'such cuteness and brazenness!'.*

> "If daughters couldn't soften a man, then nothing would."
> — Linda Weaver Clarke, Anasazi Intrigue

The man, the father, who in another world has to fight his own battles, is now his daughter's playmate, co-conspirator, and a victim of her unlimited cuteness. This is a world of their own.

> "You're going to turn into a packet of crisps
> you know that?!"
> I say.
> Laughing now.
> "No, daddy"
> She twisted her head back
> laughing in return.
> And off she skips
> back into the sitting room

having secured her prize.
Sure, how could I resist?

So what if he lost? He is a playmate and is trying his luck to morph her, you see? The father mimics playful abracadabra on the cute apple of his eye and tells her that she will turn it into a packet of crisps. A packet of crisps is the ultimate joy, for the daughter and the father, his daughter. The packet of crisps is the most loving metaphor for the crunchy love that is flowing in this poetic conversation.

She achieves her ultimate objective, the crunchy crisps. She gets back to the sitting room with her prize. The allure of the daughter's love cannot be resisted by the father. This event is a cute, curious, and cuddly way of a daughter saying 'I love you' to her father. The father returns the mushy love.

"Daddy," I whispered, feeling my own breath hitch in my throat.
"I love you."
Just when I was sure he was asleep, the one corner of his mouth
lifted in a smile. "I knew that," he murmured. "Always knew that."
— Morgan Matson, Second Chance Summer

It's a love that both know will exist forever. Such is the cosy, cute, curious world of the daughter-father's love.

The Conversations

I love talking to children. Their conversations bring us the fine experience of humanity and the wisdom of the innocent. With conditioned and scarred minds, adults are weary veterans of the world. The young are the fresh and future of the world.

The conversation with the young homie is like the ones I have with my son. The father-son relationship is different, and it is mostly advice and admonition. The little things are never there. It is about righteousness and the future. There is a definite space needed for both of us, as the young boy is growing into a man.

On the other hand, my nieces, much younger, are an unrelenting cascade of giggles, a combination of talent and cuteness, that I yearn for — as a father who had a daughter would.

Both are different worlds by themselves but united by innocence and freshness. The world needs more such conversations than busy the ones busy adults have amidst running around to make ends meet. I am blessed just for this — finding two great poems and putting them together for us to read and enjoy.

~Ashok Subramanian

8. VANITY

'If you have seen four things, I have seen sixteen', mocked my builder-client, in one of my discussions. Needless to say, I kept quiet and ended the meeting, knowing that there was no need to respond.

It was my last interaction with him. But my nightmares continued.

I wrote a short story to get it off my chest. I was overwhelmed by his panache. His vanity, albeit being a small fry in his business, was to prance like a stag and preen like a peacock — and add that slyness of fox to the mixture. I walked away from him, but it took a few days to get such overwhelming vanity off my mind.

When somebody is vain, there are lines crossed and sense disappears. Many heroes and villains have fallen because vanity was the only chink in their armour.

In a different universe, I imagine a minimalist life — where I have only those things that I need to live, and not anything by name, luxury. Modesty is always tied with minimalism, and vanity is always tied with luxury. These are inseparable. But there is an extreme form of modesty, and that denies one's existence. Such a philosophy, called '**nihilism**', considers that life itself is vain and that the end of life is the only positive element.

Vanity is the ultimate illusion. To explore the two shades of vanity — one of the materialistic nature, and the other one, which questions existence itself and says 'existence is vanity', is a tall order, but the poems demand that I step up.

Presenting '**Allure**' by Elizabeth Urabe and '**In Vain...**' by Majeed Beenteha bring a cocktail of verses that explore the deep questions hidden behind our lives, which we mask with our egos, and showcase to the world. Without much ado, let us dive into the poems.

Note: This is still a poem review and not a dissertation on philosophy.

Poem 1: 'Allure'

Figure 19 Peacock's Pomp ... Image by JL G from Pixabay

Beware pomp's allure.
  The peacock's panache is not
  proof of probity.

  ~Elizabeth R Urabe

Commentary on Poem 1:

Peacocks are considered to be majestic and proud. At a biological level, peacocks, like many males of different species, flash their tails and spread their plumes, in what is called a 'dance', to impress the female of the species. The dance and the plume are tools of courtship — the beginning of the act of progeny.

Yet, beyond the basic biological ingredient, there is a 'human quotient' in the act. The act of showing off — 'vanity'.

On the surface, vanity is a superficial attribute — almost fleeting and flashy, but there is an undercurrent to the word. The poet brings out this alluring attribute in these short yet deep verses.

Beware pomp's allure

The brief yet cautious words demand our attention. '*Pomp*' is ceremonial and spectacular, and anything that is pomp is alluring. Watch the 'Olympic games opening and closing ceremonies' or the 'march past on national days' — you will agree that the show-off, while is celebratory, is also alluring.

The underlying need is vanity. Vanity needs splendour and show-off. Vanity is never modest. It appeals to the baser senses — visual and aural, in particular. It is an extrinsic attribute. Since the fall of our senses to the allure is inevitable, the caution just about sounds right.

> "How come it can't fly no better than a chicken?' Milkman asked.
>
> Too much tail. All that jewelry weighs it down. Like vanity. Can't nobody fly with all that [stuff]? Wanna fly, you got to give up the [stuff] that weighs you down.'— Toni Morrison, Song of Solomon

There it is, the real point of function over form. Peacock is a bird that has a lot of feathers. Yet most of its tail feathers — also called plumes — are decorative. These plumes, used in spectacular displays, are the ingredients of the pomp.

Who has not fallen for a peacock's magnificence? Yet, when it comes to the main function of the feather is to fly.

Feathers form wings. Wings are organs of flight. Yet, the plumes, albeit gorgeous, are heavy. When a peacock tries to fly, it cannot reach the top of a ten feet tree. The plumes weigh them down.

Vanity is hollow, yet heavy. Vanity is attractive, yet abysmal. It can sink one, when it adorns their mental makeup, like the glittering yet heavy jewelry adorning the arms and neck of an Indian bride.

Vanity attracts baser souls. Relationships that vanity can build are very materialistic because pomp is the allure.

> The peacock's panache is not
> proof of probity.

Let us visit *'pomp'* again. The pomp of a peacock is not only in its feathers but in its tuft as well. The tuft of feathers, above its head, called *'panache'*, is ornamental mostly much like the tail.

'Panache' comes from the Latin word *pinnaculum*, which means "small wing" or "tuft of feathers." When you decorate yourself with a flourish, have an elegant appearance, or do something with style, you are said to have panache. Panache is the crown, hence is a better representation than the tail of vanity.

Vain people are insecure underneath. Insecurity leads to layers — curtains of secrecy — that lead to a lack of probity. The layers hid the truths of reality, and are normally decoys, and when peeled, the inside (or the truth) is ugly. So vainglory is nothing but superficial splendour, with underlying layers hiding the reality.

There is a crossover of the 'playful vanity' that we see in the megalomaniacal and glamorous part of our society — like in cinema or politics and there is a more serious take on the vainglory of life itself, immersed in deep philosophy. Elizabeth's poem has opened the door for a deeper discussion on Nietzschean's take on vanity. One of Nietzsche's poems talks about the vanity of peacocks. I thought it apt to bring about an extended discussion of Elizabeth's poem and Nietzsche's.

> "They learned their vanity from the sea: is the sea not
> the peacock of peacocks?
> Even before the ugliest of all buffaloes does it
> spread its tail, never becoming tired of its lace-fan
> of silver and silk.
> Disdainfully the buffalo glances, its soul near to the
> sand, closer still to the thicket, nearest, however, to
> the swamp.
> What is beauty, sea, and peacock-splendour to it! This

parable I speak to poets."
— Friedrich Nietzsche, The Poetry of Friedrich Nietzsche

I dropped the buffalo somewhere, because it is a bit offensive as is obvious, and in our line of thought, buffaloes are those who do not understand vanity.

I now proceed further on the knotting of Elizabeth and Nietzsche. Read on.

Vanity is a cloak worn by poets — using words to putting sense behind the nonsense. Poems are vain representations of the hard-hitting truth that philosophy throws up, according to Nietzsche. The verses are the poets' *'panache'*, and they flaunt them to make their point, don't they?

Have you ever heard of a modest poet? Poets are peacocks. Yet, poets are like the sea — deep in meaning, yet alluring with ornamental words such as metaphors and rhymes. I am exploring the point that even in vainglory, poets stand out as a special case, where modesty is not the best policy. So, I will let that slide.

The counterpoint is, if you the reader, think that vanity is alluring, seeing your reflection in the mirror, like the peacock, you might end up being narcissistic. Only poets can be narcissistic, Mr. Nietzsche. I will tell you why.

'But... was Narcissus beautiful?' the lake asked.

'Who better than you to know that?' the goddesses asked in wonder. 'After all, it was by your banks that he knelt each day to contemplate himself!'

The lake was silent for some time. Finally, it said:

'I weep for Narcissus, but I never noticed that Narcissus was beautiful. I weep because, each time he knelt beside my banks, I could see, in the depths of his eyes, my own beauty reflected.'

'What a lovely story,' the alchemist thought."
— Paulo Coelho, The Alchemist

I see your eyes, my dear friend; but in your eyes, I see my reflection. While you think that I appreciate the beauty of your eyes, I love my perfect image in your flawless eyes.

So when you look at a peacock (a vain person), are you another? That is vanity, mirrored. Vainglory mirrored. Narcissism, twice over.

The lake is the poet. The reader is Narcissus. The poet can sing paeans of the subject — its vainglory — but, in the verses, the poet is vanity, himself.

So, the lake or the sea is the peacock of peacocks, because it can be narcissistic or vainglorious itself, and hence, that is no proof of probity. What a paradox.

Let us get back to the buffaloes in the Nietzsche poem, now. Buffaloes are supposed to be insipid creatures. They don't understand poetry. Yet, they resemble us — the people who live life as if there is no purpose, and for whom existence is a burden. Buffaloes live their day like **nihilists**.

The burden of life is too much to bear. Life is vainglorious. Death, my dear reader, is the ultimate truth and modesty. That is what Majeed Beenteha's 'In Vain' is all about.

Poem 2: 'In vain…'

Figure 20 In vain… on this tainted stage… Image by kalhh from Pixabay

In vain, we rise — we fall — from grace
wearing out our wits on this tainted stage
and before we learn our lines in full
the curtain falls — the footlights fade.
There is no applause — no curtain calls
only an earthly plot — to mark our plight.
And all the love we gave and craved
all the broken hearts we sought to mend
falls too short — comes too late.

Alas, no prayers at Sunday church
no Hallelujahs — no cries for help
no amulets no talismans
could keep the dark chariot at bay.

~Majeed Beenteha

Commentary on Poem 2:

Who appreciates life? The best tunes are melancholy, the best verses are philosophic and they come from suffering.

From the first breath to the last, life is a journey of suffering. The only truth and the liberation from this suffering is death. Yet, people pray to live and are afraid to die. That is 'existential nihilism' at its best.

Poet Beenteha calls out the fickleness and vainglory of life.

> In vain, we rise — we fall — from grace
> wearing out our wits on this tainted stage
> and before we learn our lines in full
> the curtain falls — the footlights fade.

We make efforts to 'learn our lines'. If we have to strip life of all its vainglory, all one has to do is to exist. We create something called 'purpose', and then put efforts to achieve that purpose. The purpose could be 'internal' or 'external'.

To achieve the purpose, we *'rise and fall from grace'*. Grace, like explored before, is **poised vanity** — vanity that makes us preen like peacocks. It is like walking with stilettoes on a thin fence, and in such a tip-toed walk, we rise and fall.

The thin fence is this *'tainted stage'* of life, and the taints themselves are stains of coloured views and stereotypical perspectives of this society. To survive this 'tainted stage', we have to be on our toes, *'wearing our wits'* all the time.

Tell me this is not suffering. **It is**. This tiptoed walk on the tainted stage with our weary wits, and the fall and rise, and the walk again … I am tired, my friend, of this effort, and this pain.

> "Suffering is one very long moment."
> — Oscar Wilde, De Profundis

Indeed, life is a journey of suffering. A few years later, with what we call 'maturity' or 'experience', we must have *'learnt our lines'*, but for most of us, who are trying to get our act together, the only thing that remains is our late arrival to the party.

Death arrives much faster. The curtains of this flimsy stage have fallen, and the audience has long since left. So neither we get to perform our best, nor do the audience get to see a great performance. This fickleness of life is what makes it vainglorious and meaningless.

Of the billions of humans who lived before, how many do we remember? Does that mean that these humans did not chase purpose in their lives? Then they somewhere lost their way and ended up as ashes and dust.

> There is no applause — no curtain calls
> only an earthly plot — to mark our plight.
> And all the love we gave and craved
> all the broken hearts we sought to mend
> falls too short — comes too late.

In our lives, when we seek external validation, we are embarking on a journey of quenching our thirst from other's ponds, and so we can never have a thirst-free life. In many cases, like the billions of humans before, there is no external validation (*no applause*), and no credits (*no curtain calls*) at the end of your story. All we get, at the end of our life is an '*earthly plot*', a 6' x 3' piece, beneath which we are buried.

All the human interactions have some expectations, and by expectations, we mean purpose, and by extension, there will be disappointments and delight. The vicissitudes in their lives bring out the worst in humans, thereby questioning the spirit behind such efforts to achieve any purpose.

In our interactions, we give and get love. We have hurt and broken a few hearts and down the line, we see to mend our relationships with people. Mending fences means letting go of our ego, meaning vanity, and that comes into us a tad too late.

We have seen how our vanity and purpose make life itself vain. Such a thought, in its full form, is **Nihilism**.

> "Nihilism brings us down to earth by forcing us to confront our puniness, our failures, and our finitude. It reminds us that we are not gods, and thus helps to put us back into our appropriate place."
> — John Marmysz, Cinematic Nihilism: Encounters, Confrontations, Overcomings

Human life is fractious and unpredictable. Human minds, society, and other attributes are vain if one strips them of all the frills. Such vanity disappears when we understand that our intellectualism or evolution is our making, and it plays up to our vainglory.

We are like any other living being, who are born, live, and die. Animals, on the other hand, don't understand fame, fortune, education, and currencies. All these, which humans underline as purpose, are their creation, and if stripped, it is life at its basics that amounts to nothing. We are nothing but children of chance and misery.

"There is an ancient story that King Midas hunted in the forest a long time for the wise Silenus, the companion of Dionysus, without capturing him. When Silenus, at last, ran into his hands, the king asked what was the best and most desirable of all things for man. Fixed and immovable, the demigod said not a word, till at last, urged by the king, he gave a shrill laugh and broke out into these words: 'Oh, wretched ephemeral race, children of chance and misery, why do you compel me to tell you what it would be most expedient for you not to hear? What is best of all is utterly beyond your reach: not to be born, not to be, to be nothing. But the second best for you is — to die soon."
— Friedrich Nietzsche, The Birth of Tragedy

Given the utter shoo-down of life, is it possible to then face the ultimate truth of life — death?

Alas, no prayers at Sunday church
no Hallelujahs — no cries for help
no amulets no talismans
could keep the dark chariot at bay.

The 'dark chariot' is upon all of us. It carries us to the ultimate truth — death, which means something to all of us.

Many of us are afraid to face death, yet it is the truth. So why are we so gung-ho about life, which is a series of chance and misery, while feeling tragic and afraid of death, which is a singular event of certainty and liberation? *No prayers, songs of Hallejujah, cries for help, amulets or talisman* can prevent our escape from death, exhorts the poet.

"Disneyland remains the central attraction of Southern California, but the graveyard remains our reality."
— Charles Bukowski

The first Emperor of China, Qin Shi Huang, tried to search for the legendary Penglai Mountain in search of an elixir, but could not. He died mostly due to the very same concoction of mercury, which he drank to achieve mortality and ultimately poisoned his body.

Shi Huang's life is an example of megalomania and vainglory and serves well as an example of how existentialism can prove to be the ultimate illusion.

Not in vain:

Understanding the vanity of life is not itself in vain. Vanity is a human element and has influenced human history further and further as it evolved. Yet, sometimes, we need doses of existentialism to make life colourful, keeping aside the extensive discussion of the blandness of life (which we had just now).

> "Even nihilists put sugar in their coffee to make it sweeter."
> — Marty Rubin

Further, if life was so disinteresting and bland, humanity will itself will come to an end. 'Curiosity', a key factor for the survival and progress of the human society, will seek answers above and beyond this final understanding of life.

> "There must be no final truths; only burning questions."
> — John Marmysz, The Nihilist: A Philosophical Novel

I thank poets Elizabeth Urabe and Majeed Beenteha for sharing an opportunity with me to explore 'vanity' through their exquisite verses.

~Ashok Subramanian

9. BEHOLD, BEGET

Let us close our eyes.

Now let us think of that one person we hate. Where is the hatred coming from? Hatred, triggered by discomfort, fear, jealousy, or well, just at the looks.

Irrespective of the source, a seed is sown in our minds. The growth of this seed is fast and furious. The flame of this heat consumes our thoughts, and the poison ivy grows tall with deep roots.

The poison ivy acquires the look of a faceless fiend — a Frankenstein of our own making.

> "Most hatred is based on fear, one way or another. Yeah. I wrapped myself in anger, with a dash of hate, and at the bottom of it all was an icy centre of pure terror."
> — Laurell K. Hamilton, Guilty Pleasures

Worse, this hatred comes back from within. Raising from the deep recesses of our minds, flooding our thoughts, the faceless fiend — the Frankenstein manifests to haunt us in our nightmares.

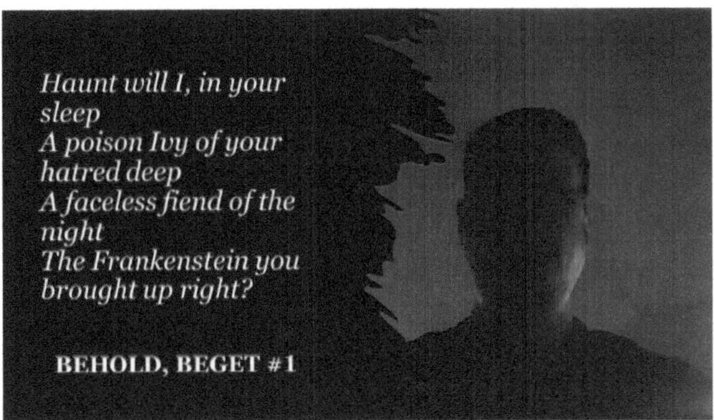

Figure 21 'Faceless Fiend of the Night' Courtesy: Ashok Subramanian

But if you have to see the person you hate in a third person, just as an observer, you will see that person smile and cry like any other person. Then where is the hatred coming from?

Let us do a simple experiment.

I decide to put myself in front of you. This is me, with my smile. I am told that a smile begets a smile.

> "A smile remains the most inexpensive gift I can bestow on any-one and yet its powers can vanquish kingdoms."
> —Og Mandino

I am not out to vanquish kingdoms, but just be me. I try to smile, at least once in a while. But with you, it has been a while, dear friend. It has indeed been a while.

I would not know that you have a fiend-me inside you, a faceless Frankenstein. Now, look at my face below. Try this with your equivalent smiling picture, if you love yours more.

That is fine. At least, you will smile back at a smiling you.

Simpler, watch yourself in a mirror and smile. You will smile back at the smiling you. Sort of begetting, right?

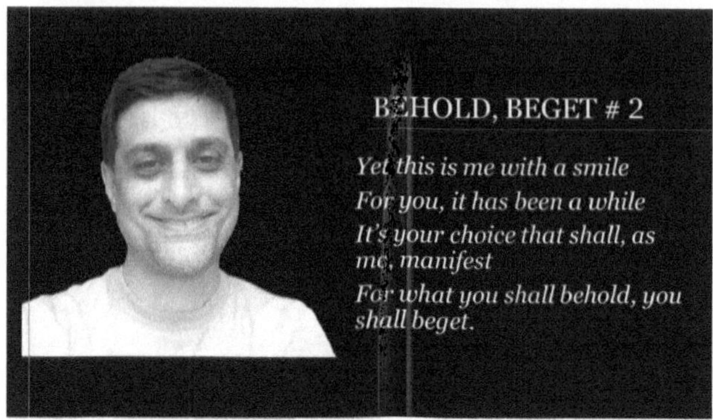

Figure 22 this is me with a smile. Courtesy: Ashok Subramanian

Finally, it is your choice. Because, whether I am a normal human with a smile or that faceless fiend that is out to haunt you in your nightmares, it is your choice.

> "Beauty is no quality in things themselves: It exists merely in the mind which contemplates them, and each mind perceives a different beauty."
> — David Hume, Of the Standard of Taste and Other Essays

Whether it is a flower or a butterfly, or a person with a smile, the beauty lies in the eyes of the beholder —you. The object that you behold, manifests in you — it begets you.

Here is the poem, therefore.

Poem: Behold, Beget

Haunt will I, in your sleep

A poison Ivy of your hatred deep

A faceless fiend of the night

The Frankenstein you brought up, right?

Yet this is me with a smile

For you, it has been a while

It's your choice that shall, as for me, manifest

For what you shall behold, you shall beget.

~ Ashok Subramanian

10. SCARS

I have a scar on my left arm. The story behind it is simple yet weird.

My brother and I were playing, and we stumbled upon a half-broken shaving blade. My brother asked me if I would feel the pain in case he cut me, and I said, I won't even know. He cut me in a flash.

A four-inch-long, half-inch wide, and half-inch deep wound opened up, my white flesh visible and blood pouring. I was unfazed by the cut. I walked to my parents, who gave me good hiding after dressing my wound.

The scar remains. While it reminds me of an innocuous, weird, and perhaps, a morbid attribute inside me, it also is a tell-tale sign of two brothers, who playfully did something dangerous.

Scars are the signatures of time on our minds and bodies. Fossils are scars. Tree trunks and rocks carry scars. Warriors — both winners and the vanquished carry scars.

Each scar tells a story. A story that evokes emotions and memories of a lifetime. Or a history lesson told in silence. If you haven't got scars, then you have not lived a life. There is no story without scars.

> "I don't want to die without any scars."
> — Chuck Palahniuk, Fight Club

What does it take a poet to relive the memories of scars? Here comes a triple-header — a treat that, I am sure, you all will lap up.

Desiree Driesenaar's 'My Scars Are Life Lines', Sakshi Arora's

'Scars', and Elizabeth Urabe's 'I have scars' explore this scary topic with panache and pain.

It does not take much time for us to jump right in. Here we go.

The first poem is about the scars that provide confidence and pride to the protagonist who is proud of her journey so far and forward.

Poem 1: My Scars Are Life Lines

Figure 23 Image by _Nini_ from Pixabay

My wounds are medals
of a life worth living.

My wounds are scars
who weave my memories
into a web of life, Life, LIFE.

My wounds are raw and real.
Lifelines I can only trace
with my thumb or my tongue.

I caress my scars and feel
how past and present

become future,
and flow
into rivers of tears
and frustrated anger.

Scars of scary moments.
Scars of heartbreak and longing,
hopelessly drowned
in impossible
dreams.

I caress my scars
and heal them.
One. By. One.

With my mind.
With universal magic.
Touched by a breeze
through the branches
of interwoven connectedness.

And when your tears join mine,
we'll decide here and now,
does it stop. Full stop?

Or shall we go on healing
and trusting each other
enough to face the risk
of new scarring
together?

Trust me
or go...

~Desiree Driesenaar

Commentary on Poem 1:

When I read this poem, I started respecting not only wounds but also other elements that leave a mark on our bodies — Wrinkles, callouses, greying hair — which are signatures of time.

The poem starts with the pride of such signatures of time, specifically wounds.

> My wounds are medals
> of a life worth living.
>
> My wounds are scars
> who weave my memories
> into a web of life, Life, LIFE.

'*Medals of a life worth living*' and '*Scars who weave my memories into a web of life, life, and LIFE*', indicate the celebration of life, and pride in such a life that goes beyond the wars that gave the scars. The protagonist of this poem has a future to look forward to, and the present that she is proud of, despite the struggles and memories.

> My wounds are raw and real.
> Lifelines I can only trace
> with my thumb or my tongue.
>
> I caress my scars and feel
> how past and present
> become future,
> and flow
> into rivers of tears
> and frustrated anger.

One day, my Facebook memories page threw up a picture of my father and me on a feed. I realized that it was the last photo of us taken together; little did I know that it would be the last photo then. I caressed the photo with my fingers as if I was holding my father's hand, and my memories with him started flooding my mind.

Such wounds, both mental and physical, can be *'raw and real'*. Dear Reader, you can also remember the moments of loss like death or separation, physical pain from a fall, fight, or an accident. The scars they leave are real and do exist. When you see the physical wound or a symbol that represents that event, you still can feel them and the pain. That is how the past rushes into the present.

The key point here is how you view those memories. As I *'trace with my thumb or my tongue'*, my senses awaken my memories, and the past becomes my present. I relive that event and feel the pain again (*'rivers of tears and frustrated anger'*). Yet, yet... they are my medals of the wars I fought and won — the fact that I am alive and here is the biggest success of my life.

> Scars of scary moments.
> Scars of heartbreak and longing,
> hopelessly drowned
> in impossible
> dreams.

Scars represent painful events. As the poet says the scars represent *'scary moments'*, *'heartbreak and longing'*, and *'hopelessly drowned in impossible dreams'* the events and outcomes.

> "Scars have the strange power to remind us that our past is real."
> — Cormac McCarthy, All the Pretty Horses

Absolutely. Scars have the power to bring the past into the present. And we cannot run away from our scars. They are the presents of the past and present in the present and also get us to be present, through our memories of the past.

> I caress my scars
> and heal them.
> One. By. One.

With my mind.
With universal magic.
Touched by a breeze
through the branches
of interwoven connectedness.

There are two ways to relive those memories. A life trapped in the past, or a life in the present and looking forward to the future, while being proud of the past. Let us tread the second path.

"Scars are not injuries, Tanner Sack. A scar is healing. After the injury, a scar is what makes you whole."
— China Miéville, The Scar

When we see our scars with pride, *'caress and heal them'*, they emerge as not remnants of the pain, but as a connection with our past, and with the universe. We live and leave prints on the multi-dimensional temporospatial realm, and we call them scars, *'caressed by a gentle breeze, blowing through the branches of interwoven connections.'*

I may go to the extent of claiming that scars can be our totem poles, carved in our bodies and minds, which we carry forward through our lives.

And when your tears join mine,
we'll decide here and now,
does it stop. Full stop?

Or shall we go on healing
and trusting each other
enough to face the risk
of new scarring
together?

Trust me
or go...

I was taken aback when these lines — but I realized that beyond the timelessness of the scars which are created by time, there is a timely call for decision.

"You should both show your scars [...] they mean you survived."
— Shelby Mahurin, Gods & Monsters

Can we share our tears and scars? If so, *'will your tears join mine?'*, *'will be facing the risk of new scarring together?'*, *'will you trust me enough?'*, asks the protagonist to her counterpart, pushing their limits, and giving the choice of either trusting her or letting go of their relationship.

Scars that are realized together are joint signatures of two souls on the fabric of space and time, and it is forged forever through trust and love.
~Ashok Subramanian

Poem 2: Scars

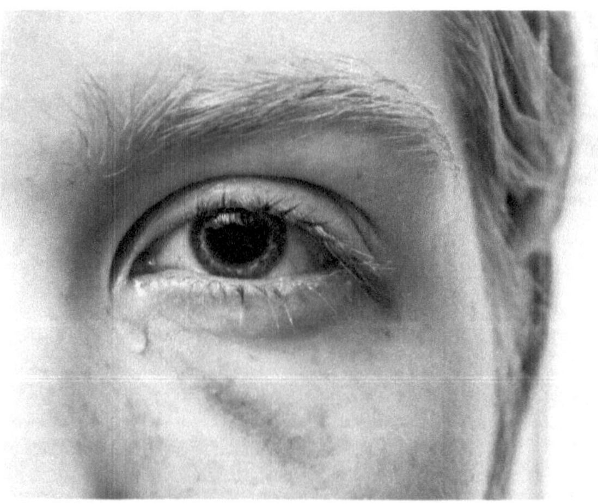

Figure 24 Image by Anemone123 from Pixabay

How can you even think of getting happiness
   after poisoning someone's life?
   How can you smile after making someone weep bit-
   terly?
   Being malicious, how can you even expect generosity?
   Disdainful heart is never regarded.
   Each drop of the bleeding heart will execrate you.

*Drop by drop the vessel of your sin will be filled
with the bitter teardrops of the one you tore apart
and it will drench you in a go.*

*I will heal my incisions
but you won't be healed.
I have learnt to call my scars 'mine'
But my scars will scare you forever.
They remember your evil face, your misdeeds, your
tortures
and my pain.
You puked hatred. Now get ready
to be choked in your own self.
Ripping up someone's petals
will leave you with only thorns.
The flowing blood of the cuts
will remind you of my bloody tears.*

*I have forgiven you for my wellbeing
But my bruises will never forget you.
It will haunt you. Curse you. Forever.*

~Sakshi Arora

Commentary on Poem 2:

Scars realized together are forged with love and trust, but some scars from deep in our souls and hearts, that are created by painful experiences of the past.

The poet recalls the painful association with her companion — either a lover or a spouse, and the breakup, and the aftermath.

*How can you even think of getting happiness
after poisoning someone's life?
How can you smile after making someone weep bitterly?
Being malicious, how can you even expect generosity?*

The poet lashes out at her ex- (that is what we will call the 'other' from here on) in anguish. One thing I have assumed about this poem is that the protagonist is a female and the antagonist is a male. It can be any other combination also, that involves love and heartbreaks.

The anguish spills into questioning the ex-'s behaviour after he has spoilt her life, living, and peace of mind. She is a wreck, and he is playing the vicious and the victim.

Just connecting back to our core theme — the protagonist is the victim (who has the scars-in-the-making), and the ex- is the perpetrator of the 'scars'.

The snapshot of time here is that the scars are 'being' made. So the concept of memories associated with scars is still to evolve. So, these outbursts from her about him are either soliloquy, yet addressed to him, or direct conversations in his presence.

He has *'poisoned her life'*, *'made her weep bitterly'*, and has *'been malicious'*. Yet he *'thinks of getting happiness'*, *'smiles'*, and *'expects generosity'*. In a heart full of hurt, the words bleed both insinuations and innuendos. His actions are abominable, and he is deriving pleasure from them. More so, the ex- is expecting her to not respond to his acts.

> Each drop of the bleeding heart will execrate you.
> Drop by drop the vessel of your sin will be filled
> with the bitter teardrops of the one you tore apart
> and it will drench you in a go.

The pain now increases as the deep effect of the wounds opens up, with the heart bleeding and the eyes spewing tears. The protagonist curses with hurting words, where each drop of blood that spills from the heart curses her ex-, and the teardrops, bitter and salty, will fill his vessel of sin and drown him.

> "So it's true when all is said and done, grief is the price we pay for love."
> — E.A. Bucchianeri, Brushstrokes of a Gadfly

The hurt of the protagonist shows here, as the curse is poetic and with shocking imagination. *'The vessel of sin will be filled by the bitter teardrops and it will drench you in a go'*, indicates the depth and volume of the sin, and that volume of bitter and salty teardrops will drench and drown the sinner.

After the Curse comes the Confidence.

> I will heal my incisions
> but you won't be healed.
> I have learnt to call my scars 'mine'
> But my scars will scare you forever.
> They remember your evil face, your misdeeds, your tortures
> and my pain.

The heart will eventually stop bleeding and the tears will dry, and the cuts — the salami slices of my heart (the protagonist says) and flesh will heal, but you — ex-, won't be healed. This piece connects with the previous poem when the protagonist calls her 'scars' proud icons of life.

The scars can also be weapons and ghosts. They can scare the sinner and the perpetrator, as they serve as totem poles of the sinner's deeds and results. Deep as the curse is, it is also filled with talent. Even the profanities are poetic indeed.

> "...to swear with a ferocity that can only be described as a talent."
> — Markus Zusak, The Book Thief

The next lines are vicious, yet strangely rhapsodic. The gruesomeness of the thoughts is enamoured by the beauty of the words. If you have watched French theatre, you can relate to mimes enacting these verses.

> You puked hatred. Now get ready
> to be choked in your own self.
> Ripping up someone's petals
> will leave you with only thorns.
> The flowing blood of the cuts
> will remind you of my bloody tears.

'Mr ex-, choke on your puke. Hatred begets hatred. The vessel of sin will drown you' — the poet displays a morbid fascination toward drenching and choking, yet the gravity of the feeling of vengeance does not escape my thoughts.

When you *'rip the petals'*, you are *'left with thorns'*. A deep, resonating thought. If somebody thought this poem was a mere rant, it disappears with this line. I have personal experience with this; When the 'human' element is removed — love, purpose et al — the underlying elements are hurting, like the thorns. When the ex- ripped her human elements, what is left shall hurt him.

> "Most women suffer thorns for the sake of the flowers, but we who wield power adorn ourselves with flowers to hide the sting of our thorns"
> — Leigh Bardugo, King of Scars

Let us not take the thorns lightly, dear friend. The ex-, in particular. The petals adorned the thorns, if you may, otherwise. The scars are the cuts by the thorns and they remind you of how you did not leave the petals on.

> I have forgiven you for my wellbeing
> but my bruises will never forget you.
> It will haunt you. Curse you. Forever.

The protagonist is liberated because she has forgiven her ex- , *'for her well-being'*. Forgiving somebody who has mortified them is not easy.

> "I could easily forgive his pride, if he had not mortified mine."
> — Jane Austen, Pride and Prejudice

But remember, the protagonist won't forget her sinner's deeds. It will *'curse and haunt him forever'*.

We see three things about scars in this poem: The Curse, The Confidence, and the Cure (Self-healing). There is the fourth element — The Cruelty. When a scorned woman is forgiving, perhaps it is not out of kindness, but out of cruelty...

"Terror made me cruel . . ."
— Emily Bronte, Wuthering Heights

Poem 3: I have scars

Figure 25 Image by JL G from Pixabay

I have scars and wounds unseen
yet my Soul remains pristine
I wend my way through life's ravine
a constant, ever changing scene

Inner mirrors must we clean
that outer world be fairly seen
Ancient secrets there to glean
newfound gems of brilliant sheen

Let not the pain of past demean
our confidence when times are lean
But rather seek the realm between
where Faith is King; Surrender, Queen

Like a peacock proudly preen
the Self's real colours, Spirit's mien
a face of ever youthful green
as Love and kindness reconvene

And from illusion's nipple wean
identity from false routine
that Truth and joy might reign Supreme
with Faith as King; Surrender, Queen.

I have scars and wounds unseen
yet my Soul remains pristine
I wend my way through life's ravine
a constant, ever changing scene...

Elizabeth R Urabe

Commentary on Poem 3:

In a world polarized, we shall look nowhere but within. The mirror does have cracks, yet we see a picture — our picture. This picture shows us the scars and wounds, yet also bares open the soul.

The '-een' rhyming poem is fresh as a teen yet celebrates the wrinkles and scars.

> I have scars and wounds unseen
> yet my Soul remains pristine
> I wend my way through life's ravine
> a constant, ever changing scene

The first thing that got my eye was the capital 'S' of the word *soul*. The respect for the inner self stands out. The inner self is pure and '*pristine*', untouched by the unseen scars and wounds. Life is throwing lemons and changing the scene constantly. With my Soul as my compass, I navigate through the maze of life.

> Inner mirrors must we clean
> that outer world be fairly seen
> Ancient secrets there to glean
> newfound gems of brilliant sheen

They say that for seeing inward, you have to close your eyes. When you close your eyes, you will visualize your thoughts, and they change scenes quickly, very much like life. The thoughts portray the outer world.

But to see your inside, you have to keep your eyes open too. Because you are reflected in the people around you. People who experience you reflect your deeds and thoughts. Yet, when you close your eyes, you will see the external world. Paradoxical?

> "For I do not exist: there exist but the thousands of mirrors that reflect me. With every acquaintance I make, the population of phantoms resembling me increases. Somewhere they live, somewhere they multiply. I alone do not exist."
> — Vladimir Nabokov

As you explore around, you learn from the old and the shining new scars. (*'Newfound gems of brilliant sheen'*). Scars are teachers, telling us stories and giving us lessons about life.

> "In a perverse way, I was glad for the stitches, glad it would show, that there would be scars. What was the point in just being hurt on the inside? It should bloody well show."
> — Janet Fitch

I wonder now how precious scars are. Let them show. Let them share their lessons.

> Let not the pain of past demean
> our confidence when times are lean
> But rather seek the realm between
> where Faith is King; Surrender, Queen

The lessons from the scars are inspiring, despite the painful story that they tell us. When we carry forward from the past to the present, we take the lessons that inspire us and the confidence that we have within.

That confidence stems from faith and love. Scars are no more open wounds, but memories of the past that inspire the present. Even in the present, when wounds are being created and we are sure that future scars will show, all we need to do is to surrender to faith and love.

> Like a peacock proudly preen
> the Self's real colors, Spirit's mien
> a face of ever youthful green
> as Love and kindness reconvene

With the mind opening to faith and love, it flowers like a *'peacock'*, that *'preens'* in resplendence, the spirit's behaviour is fresh and shows a *'face of ever youthful green'*. If you have missed it, the scars are not only teachers, but they are also vistas of openness, aided by faith and love.

> "Reason lost the battle, and all I could do was surrender and accept I was in love."
> — Paulo Coelho, The Witch of Portobello

Scars are evidence of action, and the action here is to surrender and accept love and acts of kindness. No more scars are the bitter remnants of feuds, but they are signatures of love and faith.

> I have scars and wounds unseen
> yet my Soul remains pristine
> I wend my way through life's ravine
> a constant, ever changing scene...

The inner mirrors show that the scars are imperfect, yet they teach us inspiring lessons from the past and propel us towards faith and love. The poem oozes positivity and ends with the confidence of the protagonist to navigate the constantly changing maze of life.

Scars are medallions:

> 'Scars on our skin and minds are like the stars in the sky.'

When you look at the stars in the sky, they look like mere dots that are splurged over the dark fabric above us. Yet, they twinkle and shine, each telling a story, talking to us about our past and inspiring us to our present. If our body was a universe, then the skin is the sky, and the scars are the stars.

> "If the scars of our daily reality overwhelm the beat of our life, we can at all times decide to start from square one, look up at the sky, be conscious of our pettiness, and enjoy the sparks of the stars to find the missing links. ("Man without Qualities")"
> — Erik Pevernagie

Some of the stories are painful, others are haunting, yet some are inspiring. In all, there is no life without scars, as there is no sky without stars.

~Ashok Subramanian

11. FIREFLY

Fireflies are fascinating beings — just for being able to light up the darkness and for shining their light.

In my book 'A City Full of Stories', appears a short story called 'Fireflies in a Bottle'. The Gandhari (today's Afghanistan) Princess carries fireflies in a bottle but drops them on listening to a shocking conversation with her brother. How the fireflies escape out of the broken bottle, and mix into the myriad colours that dance in the reflection of traffic lights in a puddle is the rest of the story. The transcendence from virtual originality to a metaphoric reality is the essence of that story. I wrote that story fascinated by fireflies.

Inspiring as they are, I did not get to treat them with the ode they deserve — through poems. When I searched for poems around fireflies from my usual source, LinkedIn, I landed on two gems. The poems are as fascinating as the fireflies.

Fireflies are ethereal because they defy the darkness, illuminating the space for that one moment, then another. Fireflies are magical because they add to the visions of the night. They are the equivalent of stars on earth. Even Robert Frost acknowledged that.

> Achieve at times a very star-like start.
> Only, of course, they can't sustain the part."
> — Robert Frost, The Poetry of Robert Frost

I agree on the 'can't sustain the part', yet I have a morbid affinity to fireflies, and so, will be placing them on a pedestal. The magic on earth is sometimes more enchanting than the magic of the heavens; some of us have caught those magicians in a jar — even though I don't recommend that (freedom of the fireflies, right?).

Fireflies are bioluminescent beetles. Photic emission in the adult beetle was originally thought to be used for similar warning purposes, but it is now understood that its primary purpose is in mate selection.

The interesting part is knowing that the 'glow' in the fireflies is for selecting a mate and courtship. That makes the 'fire' part of the 'fireflies' romantic.

It should be a field day for poets and romanticists. Still, I am yet to discover the 'firefly romance' poetry. I will leave it to the reader to write a poem on 'romance of the fireflies'.

Novelists and fiction authors have explored the experience — characters watching in awe the magic of fireflies, catching them in a jar, releasing them. Some explain even the gruesome side of a psycho.

> "It was as though committing murders had purged him of lesser rudeness. Or perhaps, Starling thought, it excited him to see her marked in this particular way. She couldn't tell. The sparks in his eyes flew into his darkness like fireflies down a cave."
> — Thomas Harris, The Silence of the Lambs

Don't worry. Just to bring to the fore, fireflies are fascinating even for a dark theme. That was my point, that's all.

Let us now shine some light back on them — the fireflies as seen by two poets through their poems — 'Firefly' by **Paulos Ioannou**, and an untitled quatrain by **Vineet Raj Kapoor**.

Poem 1: Firefly

Figure 26 Fireflies: Image by KIWI CHEN from Pixabay

Look at me I said, I glitter in the light,
    in every ethereal movement of my wings
    iridescent I glow coveting
    the unending sun's radiant dreams
    spellbound by the colours of the rainbow.
    I advance with that dreamy expression
    of those in love touching the blaze.
    I shatter, ignite and die.

But I am not through yet.
    More will follow,
    a battalion, marching towards the light
    always revolving
    around the vast sunlight of dreams
    and the clear vision of a new dawn.

~Paulos Ioannou

Commentary of Poem 1:

I would like the reader to consider the allowance for scientific facts.

Have you heard a firefly talk? I wonder how fireflies look at their lives. There is pleasure and pain, hope and despair in their lives.

> Look at me I said, I glitter in the light,
> in every ethereal movement of my wings
> iridescent I glow coveting
> the unending sun's radiant dreams
> spellbound by the colours of the rainbow.

The poet renders it in the first person. The poem starts with an invite to its world. 'Look at me, I glitter in the light' — a simple, yet alluring invite. The darkness on earth is like the night sky, as to how Robert Frost describes in his poem above. The stars descend as fireflies.

Their wings dazzle in *'ethereal movement'*, bringing that trail of *'iridescence'*. This is what we see.

Let me explain. For the firefly, the night is day and the day is night. In the day, illuminated by the *'unending sun's radiance'*, the fireflies are *'dazzled'* in their dreams, *'spellbound by the colours of the rainbow'*. If my night was day and you live your dreams- you are bound to be dazzled by the sun's unending radiance, and the colours of the rainbow.

The *'day-dreams'* of the fireflies inspire their nocturnal life. The signature glow is the inspiration for these daydreams. Can you see how the poet has unlocked the life of the fireflies?

> I advance with that dreamy expression
> of those in love touching the blaze.
> I shatter, ignite and die.

Most flying insects have 'positive phototaxis. It means that they are attracted to light. Their endless attraction toward light is scientifically unexplainable yet. It does not matter anyway, so let us look at this poetically.

The addiction to light attracts the fireflies. The *'advance with that dreamy expression'*. The expression is like that of a drunk human on a high, who still wants one more round. The smoothness is intoxicating, so the need for more. The radiance of the sun kicks the blissful high — the product of its 'day-dreams', and as soon as the light is visible, the phototactic beetle sways and swoons towards the bliss.

That bliss is unending love, which induces the firefly to jump into the blaze. This mad and deep love for light, which no science can explain, consumes the life of the firefly. It just *'shatters, ignites, and dies'*.

> But I am not through yet.
> More will follow,
> a battalion, marching towards the light
> always revolving
> around the vast sunlight of dreams
> and the clear vision of a new dawn.

This is not individual behavior. It is like an open season of fireflies, consumed with the blissful love *'around the vast sunlight of dreams and the clear vision of a new dawn'*.

This mass death by suicide may sound insane, yet the lives are given up wilfully, with the 'clear vision of a new dawn'. The only way the firefly can experience the new dawn is to let be consumed and devoured by the light, and we don't have a firefly yet to live and tell the tale.

It is like running towards the ledge knowing that it is a definite end, yet the thrill and promise of the 'free fall' as we plunge below are so invigorating — the moment — ah! Yet, the cauldron of white light eviscerates the body that contained the blissful soul.

Poem 2: Untitled

Figure 27 Fireflies — million lights — Image by Artie_Navarre from Pixabay

When all night, million lights fight

Sun tears apart the darkness

Even if a ray of light can tear apart the darkness,

There is a magic in a firefly's (arrogant) vigil.

~Vineet Raj Kapoor

Commentary on Poem 2:

The sun is a superpower and a villain. It can use its infinite energy and radiance to quell the dance party of the fireflies. Or the 'fight'. The orgy of the fireflies is described by the poet as a *'million lights fight'*. The little skirmishes are drunken brawls — not the soldierly ones, I dare say. Yet, the poet may differ.

The magic of the million lights that flash and vanish is in the fight. What is the fight about? The fight is to live a life in the darkness — a life of radiant bliss. The fireflies maintain an *'arrogant vigil'* over the darkness, as if, their lives depend on it. Yet, the sun, the all-powerful One, *'tears apart'* the fabric with a *'ray of light'*, and ends the glowing reign of fireflies in the night.

The beauty of this poem is that it brings out the magic and the vanity of the fireflies at the same time.

> That though they never equal stars in size,
> (And they were never really stars at heart)
> Achieve at times a very star-like start.
> Only, of course, they can't sustain the part."
> — Robert Frost, The Poetry of Robert Frost

Similar to Robert Frost's poem that I disagreed with, the vanity of the fireflies to compete with nature (*'holding the night vigil'* or trying to *'achieve a star-like start*) cannot be written off. Because, night after night, the vigil continues, only to be overtaken by the sun and the stars. Yet, there is magic, as fireflies are 'stars on earth'. This, I agree.

The Romance of the Fireflies:

When I cast my net far and wide (meaning I googled), I found poems about the romance of the butterflies. Truth be told, science suggests that the flash and glow of the night-beetles' tail is essentially a courtship dance and foreplay before a long night of love.

Here is the poem I wrote:

The Night Party

Somebody told me that

My tail is on fire

I smiled and wiggled my rear end

Only to let out a shiny flash

Somebody — my kind

Noticed the seductive wiggle

Filled with the luminescent glow

Responds in time

If only you notice

That you are at a night party

Of beetles drunk with light

No music but our buzz

An orgy of flashes

You cannot see the foreplay

Yet that is how we court

Beyond that, it is all darkness

When we copulate

Till the night party is broken

Rudely by the ruthless sun.

~Ashok Subramanian

Fireflies can be a poet's dream, and I could not refrain but join it.
~Ashok Subramanian

12. DANCE

Once upon a time, I wanted to be a millionaire.

I still do. But that is not a life goal anymore.

Today, I just want to be happy. Happiness means to dance, write, read, reflect, converse and watch. I will find my money and living style, alright.

In particular, I want to dance. I am a comic and a dud when I dance. With spidery arms and legs, and a potbelly — which I try to dissolve by intermittent running — I try to shake my neck, hips, and legs, and my family gets their dose of daily fun. My world is at peace.

Add this info — my wife is a dancer. She is a trained artist in the classical Indian dance form called 'Bharatnatyam'. As I observe her practices and performances, I can vouch for one thing — both in terms of joy and effectiveness of expressions, dance stands out as the most evolved form of human expression, because it is the visual representation of one's state of mind. (Music is a close second.)

> "Dance is the hidden language of the soul"
> — Martha Graham

A picture is more than a thousand words. An expression is more than a thousand pictures. Dance is all about expression. It speaks the language of what and who we are — our souls. It can express the full range from joy to sorrow and stoicism.

What about poetry about dance?

Dance is that magic of that fleeting moment, unlike a painting or poetry that is left to posterity to savor. Yet it is the dance that leads because living the moment is a gift, and dance is about living the moment.

Poetry about dance is about capturing that fleeting moment and rendering it to posterity. That is the magic of poetry about dance. The poet is not the poem, but the dancer is the dance. So the poetry covers the dancer and the dance. Exotic, right?

I bring together this magical capture of the present and share it with posterity through three poems. Let us shake a leg.

Poem 1: Dance is my drug of choice

Figure 28 Dance is my drug. Image by ArtTower from Pixabay

Growing up in days of disco,
    dancing is my drug of choice.

Wildly moving,
    slowly swirling,
    and daring to stare
    my admirers
    down.

Groups do scare me,
    so I grow my mask
    with intense

conversation.

The unbearable lightness of being
    has always been true for me.

But then the music
    starts to flow
    and off I go.

Perplexing the party poopers
    who thought I was shy
    who thought I was boring
    who thought I was frigid
    or frighteningly
    fierce.

Dancing is my drug of choice.

Where will the river of music
    take me
    today?

My internal stream starts flowing
    and I follow wherever
    she goes.

Vibrant vortexes accelerate
    my flow in steady beats
    and when the G-forces
    throw me out
    I land in calm water
    where my rhythmic breath
    solidifies my limbs

*and makes space
for hesitant connection.*

*Your eyes meet mine
and I drown.*

~Desiree Driesenaar

Commentary on Poem 1:

Dance is about the dancer and the dancer is about the dance. Through this poem, Desiree Driesenaar brings out the personality and emotions of the dancer.

Growing up in days of disco,
dancing is my drug of choice.

Wildly moving,
slowly swirling,
and daring to stare
my admirers
down.

Groups do scare me,
so I grow my mask
with intense
conversation.

I remember my childhood in the late '70s and '80s when Hindi, Tamil, and Telugu movies would carry songs that had a peppy beat, and the dancers would wear colourful, glittering dresses. The stage or the dance floor would be lit with colourful bulbs, rhythmically flashing, and coloured glasses reflecting rays and shadows on the dancers. It was called 'Disco'. It was not a dance, but a culture.

The famous 'smoking pipe' or the 'hookah' where one can draw the smoke in, and as it fills up the nostrils, the heady feeling brings together an eclectic bliss. Our folks called it the *'hippy'* or the '*Hare Rama, Hare Krishna*' cult, where dance and drugs went together.

The poet grew up in the '*age of disco*', like me, and no wonder if there was a heady '*drug of choice*', it was dance. I can feel the ultimate expression of inner bliss.

'*Wild moves*' and '*slow swirls*', the reference to altering speeds, and at the same time, '*dare to stare down my admirers*', indicate the exhibition of her dance talent, yet herself conscious nature.

In an environment, where hairs are down and feet are lose, the bliss yet aware nature reflects the self-preserving instinct of the dancer.

> "But here, in the great room decked out for the party, flirtation mixed with challenge and laughter with the occasional pained scream,"
> — Sarah K.L. Wilson, Dance with the Sword

A reality peep here. A flowing environment like a dance party is where wine flows, distance disappears, words flirt, bodies gyrate and lips intertwine. There are lines crossed, and in some cases, the 'self-preservation instinct' plays an important shield against any potential indiscretion.

This is a denouement and probably a misplaced exaggeration, yet I place it here with the liberty of a writer, as the '*occasional pained scream*' that may disappear in the deluge may still find the attention of a Good Samaritan.

Well, I may be wrong, as we read further verses. We will try to unravel this, so stay with me.

The dancer is an introvert. '*Groups do scare me*', she says. It is a specific trait and a situation that somebody would avoid. Yet, the dancer is there. This situation is important to realize. Doing something you are scared of. In a group, the dancer slips a mask of 'focused conversations'. That is a coping mechanism.

If there is a sense of 'self-preservation' and the 'agoraphobia' was overwhelming, why would the dancer turn up in the first place?

> The unbearable lightness of being
> has always been true for me.

The opportunity to dance is overwhelming. The discovery of *'unbearable lightness of being'*, when she dances is the reason she is on the dance floor. The feeling of lightness is without any baggage — identity, fear, guilt, or anxiety — and that liberates the dancer's mind and body.

So, the risk of coming to the dance floor, despite being agoraphobic and self-conscious, is worth it. See how it adds up. I cannot but appreciate the backstory of the dancer's presence on the dance floor.

> But then the music
> starts to flow
> and off I go.
>
> Perplexing the party poopers
> who thought I was shy
> who thought I was boring
> who thought I was frigid
> or frighteningly
> fierce.
>
> Dancing is my drug of choice.

Now coming to the act itself. '*The music starts to flow*', and '*off she goes*'.

The dance floor is surrounded by people with opinions and conformations. A fabric of conformity and bias pervades the atmosphere, intruding into the 'party ambiance'.

The party poopers, who are conformists and opinionated think the dancer is '*shy*', '*boring*', '*frigid*', or '*frighteningly fierce*'. It seems that self-conscious or self-preserving behavior might have spooked the biased minds. Yet, when she went off when the music flowed, the onlookers were '*perplexed*'. Won't they be?

Given the life of the people, anything that challenges their set patterns makes them upset. So, let us move on.

How does the dancer feel on the dance floor? She declares that dance is her drug of choice. Let us explore this drug's effect.

> Where will the river of music
> take me
> today?
>
> My internal stream starts flowing
> and I follow wherever
> she goes.

As the music injects a dose of dance into her body, she goes with the flow.

> Vibrant vortexes accelerate
> my flow in steady beats
> and when the G-forces
> throw me out
> I land in calm water
> where my rhythmic breath
> solidifies my limbs
> and makes space
> for hesitant connection.

The dancer combines speed and stillness in her movements.

'*Vibrant vortexes accelerate and when the G-forces throw me out*', indicates a heady set of twists, twirls, and turns, that flow with the beats of music, and the turn so fast that it beats gravity.

When the speed gets exhilarating, she still '*lands in calm water*', as she synchronizes her body moment with her '*rhythmic breath*'. The synchronization leads to calmness and the gyrating limbs solidify, and '*makes space for hesitant connection*', meaning, the dance creates a space for the reticent dancer so that she can deal with her inner vacillations better.

> There is a vitality, a life force, energy, a quickening that is trans-
> lated through you into action, and because there is only one of
> you in all time, this expression is unique. And if you block it, it will

never exist through any other medium and will be lost."
— Martha Graham

The creation of space and the life force through moves — twirls, twists and turns, fed by rhythmic breath and pulsating beats of music is the ultimate outcome of uninhibited dance.

Your eyes meet mine
and I drown.

In that space, where the mind is vacant, the heart is pulsating and the soul is free, the dancer's eyes meet the other, and she drowns.

Dance is the elixir of love, isn't it? As she drowns in their visual contact, sensuality is the outcome.

We shall explore how the dancer slips from a liberating dance to the one that entangles herself into a seductive amour.

Poem 2: Naked outside of Eden

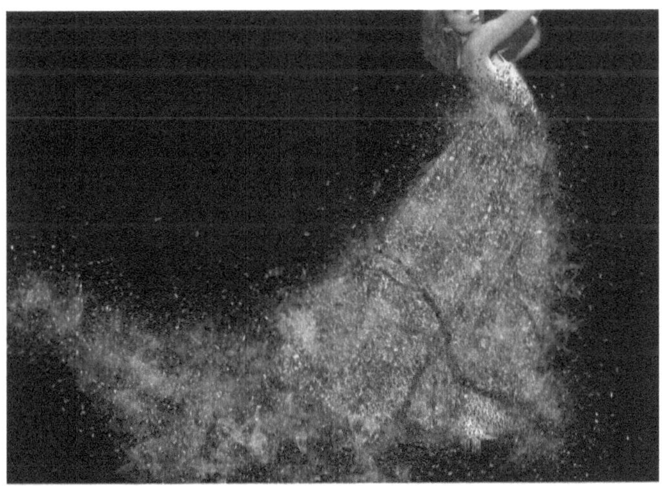

Figure 29 Naked outside of eden: image by efes of Pixabay

She is a secret thing,
    Of fantasy and dream,
    Phantom figure in the

Back corners of my mind,
Swirling dancing woman,
Eyes bright with the heat
The music and the fire
The wonder and the wine,
Timeless dancer, her face
Smiling across the flames,
And the span of time,
As she dances ancient rituals
The artlessly seductive way
Women have known since
First a man and woman
Saw and desired each other
Naked outside of Eden.

~Donovan Baldwin

Commentary on Poem 2:

Dance is the oldest art. Before humans knew how to write, paint or sing, she turned her body in a fluid motion, and there was born dance. Dance was the first tool of seduction, and the most perfect. Music, words, and pictures are younger and still to catch up.

> "Dancing is a perpendicular expression of a horizontal desire."
> — George Bernard Shaw

The expression of desire is dance. Add mystery to desire. The dancer who was 'self-conscious and crowd averse' in the first poem, now has a mysterious element around her in the second poem. The point of view now switches to that person with which she made eye contact and drowned.

> She is a secret thing,
> Of fantasy and dream,
> Phantom figure in the

Back corners of my mind

'She was a secret thing' — the opening lines add that element of mystery to the desire. The man — let us call him the 'watcher', who fantasizes and dreams about the 'dancer'.

I don't know if animals dream, but human fantasy is beastly and beautiful because there are no limits to dreams and desire. The underlying lust can flame into a poetic metaphor, raw desire wrapped in an art foil, but when a poet sees it — it is poetic lust.

The mystery of the dancer kindles the flame in the watcher, and she is this *'phantom figure of his mind'*. Her mysterious silhouette sparks the ember.

> Swirling dancing woman,
> Eyes bright with the heat
> The music and the fire
> The wonder and the wine,

'Swirling and dancing woman', is who he sees, invigorated by his desire. As he sees the flowing body in gracious moments, he is drawn to her eyes. Her eyes are *'bright with heat'* — there is a metaphor here — 'heat' reflecting her sensuous desire, and her eyes, the reflectors.

Yet, she is dancing in front of a bonfire, perhaps. *'The music'* — the pulsating beats now adding the aural component of the act, and *'the fire'*, the visual component — both the bonfire and the fire within, burning in desire and anticipation. If that is not enough, we see the *'wonder and wine'*, the alcohol adding fuel to the *'flame'*.

> "Either give me more wine or leave me alone."
> — Rumi

The power of wine, pure and subtle, remains in the background, yet provides sublime titillations to the senses that are already tuned to the fire, music, and dance.

Timeless dancer, her face

> Smiling across the flames,
> And the span of time,
> As she dances ancient rituals

'Timeless dancer' originates from 'timeless dance'. It is the art known to humans even before they spoke — see the peacocks and the beetles, they dance to mate.

Dance is the foreplay. Such an art, spans all creatures, making it the only art that all creatures can perform. So, timeless it is the art itself, and timeless she is, the performer.

She smiles, knowing that she is good and knowing what she wants. Her smile fans the flames, themselves crackling in laughter. Her movements are timeless and ancient, as we have seen.

> The artlessly seductive way
> Women have known since
> First a man and woman
> Saw and desired each other
> Naked outside of Eden.

Can art be artless? I think so. The wink and glare of an eye, the inviting smile, and the gesture or gyration that does not fit into a textbook dance, yet conveys a real meaning that strips the charades of civility, betraying the raw emotion, then art can be artless.

> "And there was something so artless in this smile that I had to smile back."
> — James Baldwin, Giovanni's Room

The invite which is artless does get a response back.

For that was how *'first a man and woman saw and desired each other naked outside of Eden'.* As much as the veils of civility are reaped apart, a desire that is raw, yet rich, flows between the two passionate souls — the dancer and the watcher.

While the act outside Eden gets erotic, how about some self-love?

Dance is soup for our souls. If you are searching for salvation or solace, dance is the best companion.

Poem 3: Let Dance Command

Figure 30 let dance command: Image by cocoparisenne at Pixabay

Play some soul
   Start to sway
   Turn it up
   All the way

Close your eyes
   let all go
   Unlock the dancer
   in your soul

Freedom flows
   as you dance
   Magical
   Is this trance

Music rhythm
   Funky beats

> Souls on fire
> happy feet
>
> Alluring twists
> Swinging hips
> Synchronizing
> curled up lips
>
> Potent power
> Clapping hands
> Uplifting tempo
> Big bop bands
>
> Sliding floors
> as with slippers
> Graceful arms
> Tingling shivers
>
> Countless people
> with commotion
> Let dance command
> your locomotion
>
> Lord have mercy
> this is bliss
> Spirits rise
> Feeling massive
>
> Worries leave
> as does fear
> Provoking dance
> makes you cheer

Anytime
*   you're feeling blue*
*   Summon up*
*   This power shoe*

Ancient movements
*   Beat enhanced*
*   there is healing*
*   when you dance*

~Paula Goodman

Commentary on Poem 3:

This poem is a simple way of how to dance.

Play some soul
Start to sway
Turn it up
All the way

Close your eyes
let all go
Unlock the dancer
In your soul

It is that simple. The words of these verses and the steps to dance. All you have to do is to listen to music that appeals to your music, and then sway with it. The idea is to let the music seep in, and embrace the dancer within you.

Music rhythm
Funky beats
Souls on fire
happy feet

Alluring twists

Swinging hips
Synchronizing
curled up lips

Dance to the rhythm of the beats. Have you seen your feet happy? Then dance. Set your souls on fire.

Swing and twist your hips, and mime the song in your curled lips. See it is that simple.

"Nobody cares if you can't dance well. Just get up and dance.
Great dancers are great because of their passion."
— Martha Graham

Have you begun? Now you just dance. Dance. When you let the music lead, and you follow with your heart, you master the art.

Potent power
Clapping hands
Uplifting tempo
Big bop bands

Sliding floors
as with slippers
Graceful arms
Tingling shivers

Countless people
with commotion
Let dance command
your locomotion

Now, look around. Do you see the dance floor and the music band? As you dance, they clap, lifting the tempo and perhaps, reaching a crescendo for each song that is belted out by the disco jockey or music band. The crescendo brings shivers, the feeling of exhilaration. The excitement draws 'countless people' and 'commotion. The poet suggests that you keep the focus — the dance shall command your moves.

Lord have mercy
this is bliss

    Spirits rise
    Feeling massive

    Worries leave
    as does fear
    Provoking dance
    makes you cheer

    Anytime
    you're feeling blue
    Summon up
    This power shoe

When I write this piece, it is already Christmas. That time of the year, when peace and quiet engulf us. So, praise the Lord that He has mercy upon us that this blissful time of Christmas continues. The spirit of life stems from hope and happiness.

Let us all keep our worries and fears in a closet, and let our feet lose and hair down, that shall cheer us and the people around us. Anytime you feel the blues, put on your dance shoes.

Such a simple 'swaying to the music', brings the art and answers out of us.

Dancers are the answers

> "Dance, when you're broken open. Dance, if you've torn the bandage off. Dance in the middle of the fighting. Dance in your blood. Dance when you're perfectly free."
> — Rumi

Dance is the go-to therapy for happiness and sorrow, for the highs and the lows, for bondage and freedom, in war and peace.

Seduce life through dance.

Your life is your dance. You are the dancer.

~Ashok Subramanian

13.   THE DAYS AFTER

I looked at the grey cloudy skies. It was one of the last days of December 2021.

I don't remember the date. I don't need to.

I have been counting the days since I immersed my mother's ashes in the endless ocean.

The grey clouds decided to cry with salt-less tears and holler through thunder rolls. As it turned out, they sobbed and sobbed, for almost six hours.

Were they crying their heart out? Good for them.

I had cried too. Even though it was the end of the rainy season, such a cloud burst was not expected. But these rains were different- the first rains during *the days after*. For the first time, I felt my mother's tears from heaven.

The year 2021 would be recorded in memories as the year I lost my mother. We thought she would pull through till New Year, but given what she underwent, we felt that her passing away earlier was the best thing that happened to her. Less pain in living and freedom in death.

Figure 31 my mother: — 2021. The photo was taken in 2019.

Today, it is a month since, yet I feel that she lives on like the images of shattered glass, in my memories and pictures that we come across. Of course, she has a special permanent home in our hearts, and out there, in the heavens.

The days after her passing away have not been easy. We still hear her voice and feel the wrinkles of her soft, loosened flesh, which I had set fire with teary eyes.

I dedicate this article to my mother. Now to *the days after*...

As I venture with trembling fingers and heavy heart to type this poetry review — the last for the year 2021, I choose two young poets, Sakshi Arora and Bishal Dey, both of whom I adore to capture the essence of my 'days after.'

The person that we mourn or pine for is not around anymore, but the memories, feelings, and aches —are all there.

The first poem is about the loss of a lover and her heart. The pain is imminent and inevitable, yet the expression of anguish is still relevant because the words of longing and languishing will be immortal.

The days after the love is lost, are long and lonely.

Love is not only between two lovers, but it can also be with a family. A family is built on blood relationships — sanguinary —

but also love. Love is the fulcrum of the family, and when a family member goes to forever-land, the surviving members have to pick up the pieces.

Poem 1: Take me along

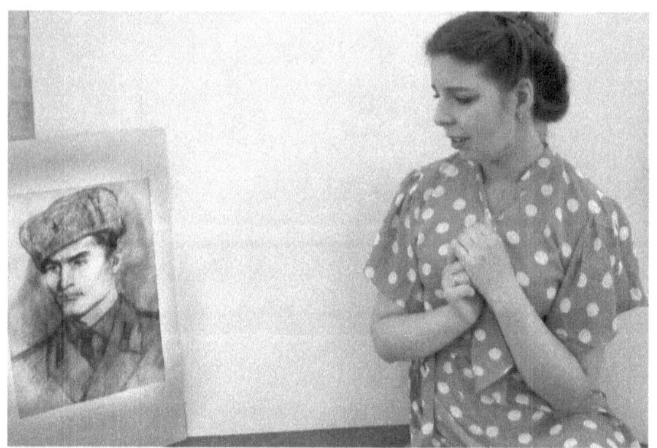

Figure 32 Picture by ReneEstok of Pixabay

You left my world and this world left me.

In this journey of life, you got a new destination

And my heart lost its way.

Take me along with you, darling;

I'm lost alone without you.

You gave this heart such a pang of pain,

I'm breathing with a dead soul.

I don't want to live in this heartless ruthless world

These silent teary eyes are calling you.

Come back, love! Take me along with you.

There is dark emptiness in my heart

Hold my hand! I will drown in my stream of sorrow.

Merciless Pitiless world is playing with my ripped heart

Look around! There is nothing but a ravaged ruined world.

I am still yours! Take me along with you.

~Sakshi Arora

Commentary on Poem 1:

The poet laments about her missing lover. Fate had played spoil-sport in their lives. She yearns to be with him, even if he has crossed over to another realm.

> You left my world and this world left me.
>
> In this journey of life, you got a new destination
>
> And my heart lost its way.
>
> Take me along with you, darling;
>
> I'm lost alone without you.

Her world has crashed — she feels like floating in space without gravity, and nothing to hold on to. His love was her life's crutch. When love blossomed, her heart leaned on his, like how plants lean towards the sun. Love nourished her growth, and suddenly the lover was missing. Her lover is dead, but her love is not. She is seeking it back from him, and for that, she wants him to take her along.

Of course, he cannot take him with her. He is gone. Yet she implores him. She feels alone and lost. What to do next? They were so ensconced in their cozy love that a life with him is rudderless for her.

> You gave this heart such a pang of pain,
>
> I'm breathing with a dead soul.
>
> I don't want to live in this heartless ruthless world
>
> These silent teary eyes are calling you.
>
> Come back, love! Take me along with you.

Let us imagine that we are suddenly waking up from a dream, and the real world rushes into our senses and minds. The feeling is overwhelming and our heartaches and head throbs. Maybe, there are palpitations even.

His sudden leaving opened her up to reality. In the harsh, cold world, she just living with a dead soul. A soul without the emotions of the heart. She implores them to take her away from this world and to their vicarious safety — a cosy, cocooned with the warmth of his love.

> There is dark emptiness in my heart
>
> Hold my hand! I will drown in my stream of sorrow.
>
> Merciless Pitiless world is playing with my ripped heart
>
> Look around! There is nothing but a ravaged ruined world.
>
> I am still yours! Take me along with you.

His presence was real. His love was real. So her world was real AND caring. That real world ceased to exist and brought the 'real' world — merciless, pitiless, ravaged and ruined, a world that does not put 'love and care' over everything else — back in.

She senses his presence as if he has come back, or rather he has never gone away; It is a sense of denial and her conversation with that imagery is built on the sense of denial. She beseeches him to hold her hand and look around the cruel world around her. She reminds him that she was still his.

> "It's difficult for me to imagine the rest of my life without you.
> But I suppose I don't have to imagine it… I just have to live it"
> — Ranata Suzuki

Then she says, '*Take me along with you.*' That is more of a cry of anguish. The reality has already begun to set in — where, the lonely, harsh world will be her living place, and his memories will be the balm on the wounds inflicted by her habitat.

The poet stitches the torn fabric with the sutures of loving memories, she also indicates the multi-dimensional nature of such an emotion. When love is lost and life moves forward, it is a journey that nobody would want to take.

That love also rips the life, heart, and soul of a dependent — the mother and the wife. The second poem by **Bishal Dey** brings out the agony of a widow, who has spent her life running the household, taking care of the needs of her husband and son. The loss of her husband unhinges her bearings and the verses paint a poignant picture.

Poem 2: The Thing No One Asks

Figure 33 Picture by cocoparisienne of Pixabay

He lay on his bed
   when suddenly a sharp shrill voice reaches his ear.
   He sat silently in a room.
   When he again heard the sharp shrill voice.

The voice was that of a broken heart.
   The voice was of someone who has found her love and
   then lost him.
   Time went by but tears remained.
   Someone cried with a hollow chest.
   Repeating the same lines

Maybe someone stitched her feelings within her.
   Not able to say it all.
   And whatever she would say not most could get it.
   Rolling with pain she wishes for death.
   She keeps speaking about her mistakes
   that she never made.

Her eyes have swollen.
   She watches the night turn day
   she has forgotten what a day looks like
   Fear has got her in between its hand.

She is vulnerable her tears wet her son's vest.

An unknown future of uncertainty now waits.
  As she and her family now lives with fear, anxiety, vul-
  nerability and uncertainty.
  Let them hope it's all good for them ahead.

  ~Bishal Dey

Commentary on Poem 2:

The visuals that this poem presents are what I noticed first.

The visuals start with the son and move on to the mother. From the mother, the camera moves towards a setting sun. I took my time to understand the poem so that I don't miss the vitality of the imagery while holding brimming emotions.

> He lay on his bed
> when suddenly a sharp shrill voice reaches his ear.
> He sat silently in a room.
> When he again heard the sharp shrill voice.

The father is gone. The son lit the pyre at the cremation site, while far away, her mother was still sobbing in the agony of her husband's loss. Everyone who had come for the last rites has left.

The quiet descended in the house — a house without the father. The son and the mother now stay unable to reconcile with the fact that the breadwinner and on who they were dependent is not there anymore.

The weight of silence is unbearable. He lies there, and hears a 'sharp shrill voice' — the voice of his mother pierces the silence and into his ears. The silence is an intermission in their lives, but now, the reality has started sinking in — which is announced by the 'sharp shrill voice'.

> The voice was that of a broken heart.
> The voice was of someone who has found her love and then lost

> him.
> Time went by but tears remained.
> Someone cried with a hollow chest.
> Repeating the same lines

The shrill voice brings to open the wounds of *'the days after'*. His mother loved his father but not in a typical way. She was the quiet young girl who married a stranger and was asked to go to her husband's house filled with strangers who she called in-laws. She had to serve him, and all of them, without a word. From cooking and cleaning to massaging his tired limbs when he returned to work.

In that insipid life, there was a special connection between them, for he took care of her needs, remembering her beyond his tiring day's work and the patriarchy that prevailed in and around him. Such love is quiet because there are no poets to write about it, yet the love finds its dwelling in the heart of a demure woman and a quiet man.

There was no fire between them, but the love itself was like the embers of a bonfire, quiet yet crackling. This was the sort of love she had found.

The patriarchy withered away, the previous generations gone, her generations have left since, yet they lived and loved in their home. She bore a son, a symbol of their quiet love.

Now, her love was gone. In a sudden twist of fate, she lost him to the embers of flames. Only his memories remain.

The memories kindle her fear and anguish, and she cries and hollers, in her shrill voice, till her chest has become empty. She repeats the same words, lamenting and painful, and tears wash over them. Time, for now, did not appeal its proverbial balm.

> Her eyes have swollen.
> She watches the night turn day
> she has forgotten what a day looks like
> Fear has got her in between its hand.
> She is vulnerable her tears wet her son's vest

Her eyes swell like a tearful rose, red and all; through the curtain of tears, she sees the cycle of time turn between day and night. Given that she has been sitting in the corner, impervious to the time that passed, her mind is paralyzed in the aftermath of her husband's demise.

Her son who stayed away, giving her space for mourning and recovery, goes to her. She leans on him, her son, the outcome of their love. Her tears now wet his vest — the weather is humid, and the men wear vests at home. His chest gives her the cushion to soak her tears, and the bulwark of her life from thereon.

> An unknown future of uncertainty now waits.
> As she and her family now lives with fear, anxiety, vulnerability and uncertainty.
> Let them hope it's all good for them ahead.

The family — she and her son, now grown up, still will have to live with an uncertain future. The poet wishes the family well.

The Days After

> "Ever has it been that love knows not its depth until the hour of separation."
> — Kahlil Gibran

When the phone call came from my brother, I wish that I had not picked up the phone. He said 'Amma...'

'I am starting right away.' I said and kept the phone down.

During her days at the hospital, she had made me play songs that would squeeze our hearts with aches. She would call me every day, just to ask me if I ate.

After that call, I told myself it was not real; but I knew it was. I saw her serene and peaceful face, eyes closed, forever. For the first time, I realize that I was an orphan. I was an adult, had my own family, seen success all over, yet I was an orphan.

My brother and I did our usual thing — we went out for a long walk in the small hours of that morning, while she slept forever, at our home, in an icebox. We talked about our childhood and her, and tears flowed. We realized our love for each other, as brothers, as parent and children, and as family.

The poems bring out the pain of that forever loss, and the days thereafter. It is an ending that nobody wants, but as they say, life goes on. A page turns. On that page, a story would be written without the loved one, whose life hit a full stop on the previous page.

~Ashok Subramanian

PONDER 2021: FEATURED POET BIOGRAPHIES

SHWETA HITESH JOSHI

Shweta Hitesh Joshi is a published poet. Her collection 'Verses of the Universe' was published in January 2022. Her editing and creative advising works include 'Ponder 2020', 'A City Full of Stories' and 'Planned Pandemic 2020.' She is a voracious reader. She lives in Bengaluru/ Milan, Italy. Before her literary journey, she was an HR and business consultant.

BISHAL DEY

Bishal Dey is a pharmacy student and writes poems on LinkedIn. Ponder 2021 is his first published work. He lives in Siliguri, India.

DESIREE DRIESENAAR

Desiree Driesenaar is a polymath. She is a poet, abundanist, and regenerative solutions, expert. She is a champion writer in multiple publications and forums including The Illuminated, Medium (her blog), and BizCatalyst 360. Her book on Abundanism is expected shortly. She lives in Venlo, Limburg, Netherlands. Desiree, Elizabeth, and I, for,m a special connection called our 'tribe'.

ELIZABETH (BETH) URABE

Elizabeth Urabe is a Spiritual Midwife or Spiritual Art Medium. She is a poet who uses few words and packs a spiritual punch, reaching our souls directly. Her Urabe Batik designs are world famous – they connect with you in different forms depending on where and how your soul perceives them.

She lives in the highlands of Arizona. Desiree, Elizabeth, and I form a special connection called our 'tribe'.

SAKSHI ARORA

Sakshi Arora is a master in English Literature and a published poet. Her book 'Aisling' is an amazing collection of fresh poems. The poems that appear here are part of the book. She lives in Prayagraj, Uttar Pradesh, India.

PAULA GOODMAN

Paula Goodman is a Poet, Word Jedi, Writer, and Editor. She is also a certified Yoga Teacher. She is a Featured BizCatalyst 360 contributor. She brings her experience in customer service, financial services, team management, and word Jedi magic into her writings. She is currently self-employed at 'Omathome'. She lives in Hamilton, Ontario, Canada.

VINEET RAJ KAPOOR

Vineet Raj Kapoor is an India expert (Industrial Design Technology) in Worldskills International. He is a passionate designer and design mentor and believes that gamification in design can help society. Over the years he transfused into an Artist, Engineer, Writer, and Designer. His poems are short and deep. He lives in Chandigarh, India.

PAULOS IOANNOU

Paulos Ioannou is a prolific and published poet. He writes on LinkedIn and has contributed to 18 publications. He was the chair coordinator for the Planning Group for the International Day of People with Disabilities on behalf of the City of Toronto between 2005 and 2010. He lives in Toronto, Ontario, Canada

ASHOK SUBRAMANIAN

Ashok Subramanian is a prolific and published poet and fiction author. He publishes his poetry under the 'Poetarrati' title and has published three volumes. He writes fiction, poetry, and book reviews. He is a management graduate from IIM Calcutta and is an engineering graduate. He lives in Chennai, India.

BEE-N-TE-HA BEENTEHA

< Photo not available >

Majeed Beenteha's poetic work is often dark portraying pain, dislocation, and trauma. Moving back and forth between Tehran and New York City, Beenteha's photography work projects a sharp contrast between traditional and modern realities that co-exist uneasily in modern-day Iran. Beenteha's work often features Iranian women dressed in an iconic fashion that seems more sacred than profane. He is a filmmaker, music composer, photographer, and poet. He lives in New York City.

YASMIN ADEN

Yasmin is a passionate poet who writes poetry on LinkedIn. Ponder 2021 is one of her first publications. She is a management graduate from the Islamic University of Kenya and is open to work. She lives in Nairobi, Kenya.

KEN HUME

Ken Hume is a freelance blogger and spoken word artist. He launched his first collection of poetry in 2011 'Snowstorm of Doubt and Grace' and currently working on his second poetry collection "What Happened Next" (2019 update). He wrote film & gig reviews for a local paper called the Tullamore Tribune from December 2005 – to September 2008. He lives in Offaly Country, Ireland.

DEEPSHIKHA SHEKHAWAT

Deepshikha is a poet while studying for her bachelor's degree in Ayurvedic medicine. She is a content writer and writes on medium.com. Ponder 2021 is one of her first publications. She lives in Jodhpur, Rajasthan, India.

PRIYA PATEL

Priya's poems search for and explore human minds and emotions. She has more than 20 years of experience in customer service and the hospitality industry. She lives in Big Spring, Texas, United States.

ALLISON ROSE CLARK

Allison is the author of 'I Don't Hate Me Anymore', which is a unique combination of self-improvement and autobiography. She successfully graduated with a Diploma in Counselling, and Certificate IV in New Small Business. She lives in Wollongong, New South Wales, Australia.

AKINKUNMI AKINBODE ET ADEBANKEMO ODUGUWA

Akinkunmi Akinbode is a poet, content and SEO writer, brand storyteller, and digital artist. His poems paint a picture of life around him. He is based in Nigeria.

Adebankemo Oduguwa is a trained veterinarian, writer, Innovation strategist, purpose and Creativity Coach @Omnipurpose; and CEO @D'sfoodanimalkonceptz. She co-wrote the poem presented in Ponder 2021. She lives in Idaho, USA.

SOURABHA RAO

Sourabha Rao is a professional writer, poet, translator, and freelance columnist with literary proficiency in English and Kannada and over six passionate years in environments of excellence. She has contributed editorial articles to Deccan Herald and several Kannada newspapers, currently authoring a weekly column in Vishwavani. She has been long-listed for the Toto Awards for Poetry in Kannada and English. She lives in Bengaluru, India.

DONOVAN BALDWIN

Donovan Baldwin is a seventy-six-year-old U.S. Army retiree. He is a poet and article writer having published several poems in small literary journals and has over 400 articles published on various websites. He is also a past member of Mensa. He is an ABO Certified Optician. He lives in Fort Worth, Texas, USA.

ADEDOYIN OLALEYE

Adedoyin is an award-winning poet, creative writer, author, microbiologist, and epidemiologist. She has won the World Poetic Star issued by the World Nation Writers' Union in August 2019 for her works of excellence in the field of world literature. She lives in Lagos, Nigeria.

PARNEET KAUR

Parneet Kaur helps DTC brands leverage their social media. She is a content marketer and copywriter. Ponder 2021 is one of her early publishing. She lives in Bengaluru, India.

THE END

---

[1] https://www.nationalgeographic.com/animals/birds/facts/cardinal#:~:text=Cardinals%20are%20fairly%20social%20and,eggs%E2%80%94typically%20three%20per%20season.

[2] https://author-ashok.medium.com/poem-review-time-2c44dca0209